Contents

Place value

Revise wise

We use ten digits to make all our numbers:

0 1 2 3 4 5 6 7 8 9

The key thing to learn is that the position of these digits gives numbers their value:

millions	hundred thousands	ten thousands	thousands	hundreds	tens	units	
						5	five
					5	0	fifty
				5	0	0	five hundred
			5	0	0	0	five thousand
		5	0	0	0	0	fifty thousand
	5	0	0	0	0	0	five hundred thousand
5	0	0	0	0	0	0	five million

Read this number aloud: 63 450

Check it: sixty-three thousand, four hundred and fifty.
Did you notice that there is a pause after you say the word 'thousand'? This pause is sometimes shown by a **space**: 63 450, and sometimes by a **comma**: 63,450.

This will help...

Reading numbers bigger than 10000 can be tricky. Put a space in front of the hundreds and read them in groups of thousands:

362495
↓
362 495
↓
362 thousand 495

Try reading these headlines:

£795693 jackpot win for bingo-playing Granny!

14 267 wigs stolen – police are combing the area

Man eats 203,184 baked beans – breaks world record

Try these

1 Write the number 92 034 in words.
2 Write the number one hundred and twenty thousand, six hundred and four.
3 Which number is 1 more than 64 099?
4 What is the value of the 2 in the number 72 450?

If you know your stuff...
45 367
46 753
37 645
62 374
...you'll spot the odd one out.

Look at the position of each digit for their value

148 625 = 100 000 + 40 000 + 8 000 + 600 + 20 + 5

Puzzle code

Which number is four hundred and six thousand, nine hundred and twenty three?

4 006 923 (C) 406 923 (O) 460 923 (T) 469 023 (M)

Write the letter in the grid on page 64.

 On your toes What is the next odd number after 999?

10s, 100s and 1000s

Because of our clever number system, to multiply and divide by 10, 100 or 1000 you just follow some simple rules.

Multiply by 10

Move the digits **one place** to the **left** and fill the space with zero.

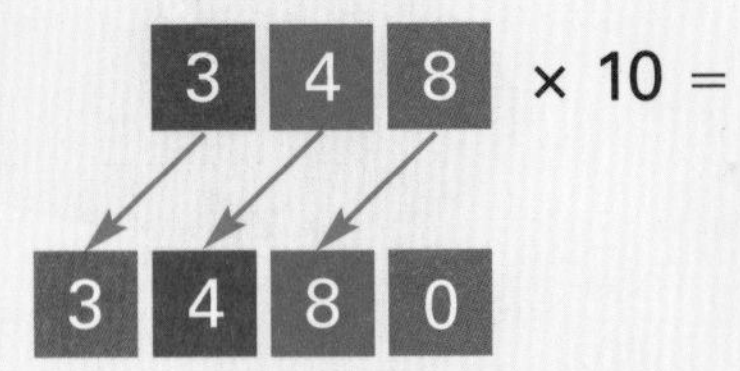

Multiply by 100

Move the digits **two places** to the **left** and fill the spaces with zeros.

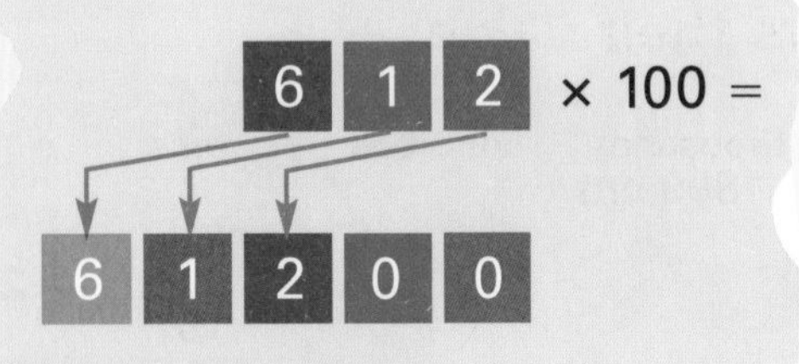

Multiply by 1000

Move the digits **three places** to the **left** and fill the spaces with zeros.

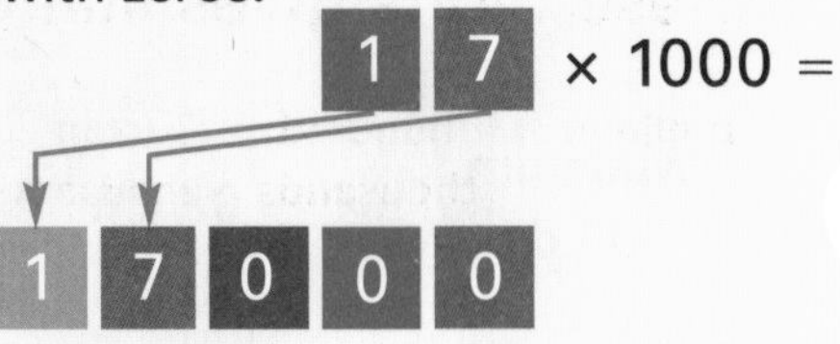

Divide by 10

Move the digits **one place** to the **right**.

1 2 3 0 ÷ 10 =

1 2 3

Divide by 100

Move the digits **two places** to the **right**.

6 1 0 0 ÷ 100 =

6 1

Divide by 1000

Move the digits **three places** to the **right**.

3 8 0 0 0 ÷ 1000 =

3 8

This will help...

If you need to divide or multiply by 20, 50, 300, 400... or any multiple of 10 or 100, sort the zeros out first.

So...

342 × 20 is 3 420 × 2 → 6840

2 150 ÷ 50 is 215 ÷ 5 → 43

If you know your stuff...

61 .... 610 ... 6100 .... 61 000 .... 611 000

...you'll spot the odd one out.

1 314 × 100 = ?

2 Which number is 10 times smaller than 6020?

3 385 × ? = 385 000

4 ? ÷ 100 = 471

Multiplying by 10, 100 or 1000 moves the digits to the left.

Dividing by 10, 100 or 1000 moves the digits to the right.

Puzzle code

Centipedes and millipedes don't really have 100 legs or 1000 legs. The world's biggest centipede only has 46 legs. Some millipedes have ten times this number which is:

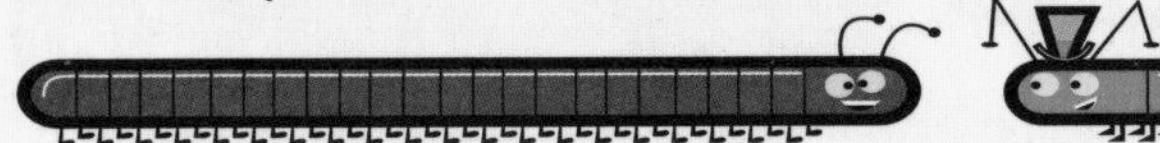

406 **(D)** 4 600 **(A)** 460 **(N)** 400 **(M)** *Write the letter in the grid on page 64.*

On your toes Write this number: six hundred and seven thousand, three hundred and eighteen.

Comparing numbers

Revise wise

Putting numbers in order can be tricky if they don't all have the same number of digits.

To make absolutely sure of the order, write the numbers underneath each other, lining up the units digits.

'Chucking the Welly' is a very important event in the Piddlewick Village Fete. Here are some of the distances thrown:

Malcolm	Sue	Bill	Alex	Kate	Ron
803 cm	98 cm	1809 cm	614 cm	2014 cm	2026 cm

Can you put the distances in order?

First write the distances under each other.

803
98
1809
614
2014
2026

REMEMBER LINE UP THE UNITS

Now put them in order. Compare the thousands first, then the hundreds, tens and units:

2026
2014
1809
803
614
98

< means is less than

For example,
278 **<** 287 means
278 is less than 287

> means is greater than

For example,
309 **>** 278 means
309 is greater than 278

This will help...

If you are asked to put amounts of money or measures in order, change them all to the same unit. For example, if you need to put 1804 cm, 18 m and 84 m in order, first change them all to centimetres: 1804 cm, 1800 cm and 8400 cm. Now it will be a bit easier to order them.

Try these

1. Put these numbers in order, starting with the smallest: 7645 7066 769 1997 1809
2. Which is the larger number, 14006 or 1507?
3. Which sign is missing, < or >? 2344 ☐ 2334
4. Give three numbers that could go in the gap: 62110 < ___ < 62121

If you know your stuff...
314 > 310
90123 < 9300
4006 > 599
6987 > 14300
...you'll spot the odd one out.

To compare numbers, look at the digits: start from the left and work your way to the right.

Puzzle code

A < B < C

A is 200 less than B, and B is 300 less than C. What is the difference between A and C? 100 **(B)** 200 **(A)** 500 **(C)** 300 **(R)**

Write the letter in the grid on page 64.

 On your toes Jupiter is almost 10 times bigger than Venus (diameter 12 103 km), what is Jupiter's diameter?

Approximating numbers

Revise wise

There are times when you don't want to work with exact numbers – an approximate answer is all you need.

To do this, **round** the numbers to the nearest ten, hundred or thousand.

Rounding to the nearest 10

Look at the units digit, if it is:

- ★ 5 or more, round up the tens digit
- ★ less than 5, the tens digit stays the same.

62**6** rounds **up** to 630
57**4** rounds **down** to 570

Rounding to the nearest 100

Look at the **tens** digits, if it is:

- ★ 5 or more, round up the hundreds digit
- ★ less than 5, the hundreds digit stays the same.

61**5**4 rounds **up** to 6200
36 5**2**8 rounds **down** to 36 500

Rounding to the nearest 1000

Look at the **hundreds** digit, if it is:

- ★ 5 or more, round up the thousands digit
- ★ less than 5, the thousands digit stays the same.

41 **6**35 rounds **up** to 42 000
87 **3**49 rounds **down** to 87 000

This will help...

When you work out an approximate answer to a tricky calculation, you need to know whether it is best to round the numbers to the nearest 10, 100 or 1000. For example, 738 × 89 rounded to the nearest 10 is 740 × 90, which is still a bit difficult to work out in your head. So rounding to the nearest 100 is better: 700 × 100 is 70 000.

37 588 people flew with the airline 'Hot Air' last year. This year there were 65 299 passengers.

Approximately how many more people flew with 'Hot Air' this year?

37 588 → to the nearest 1000 → 38 000
65 299 → to the nearest 1000 → 65 000

65 000 – 38 000 = 27 000

So approximately 27 000 more people flew with 'Hot Air' this year.

≈ means is approximately equal to

65 299 – 37 588 ≈ 27 000

Try these

1. What is £43 685 rounded to the nearest £100?
2. What is 36 464 g rounded to the nearest 1000 g?
3. 3285 x 99 ≈ ____
4. What is the approximate total of 3689 and 7084?

If you know your stuff...

2634 → 2600
3197 → 3200
5765 → 5770
6854 → 6900

...you'll spot the odd one out.

Round a number to the nearest 10, 100 or 1000.

1500
1450
1400

If it is in the middle round it up

Puzzle code

6156 Roman coins are found in equal numbers in 19 leather bags. Approximately how many coins are in each bag?

300 **(E)** 3000 **(A)** 500 **(L)** 200 **(M)**

Write the letter in the grid on page 64.

On your toes What is the missing number? 3799 < ____ < 3801

Negative numbers

Revise wise

Negative numbers are numbers below zero.

Numbers above zero are called positive numbers.

This is easy to see if you imagine a number line carrying on backwards past zero:

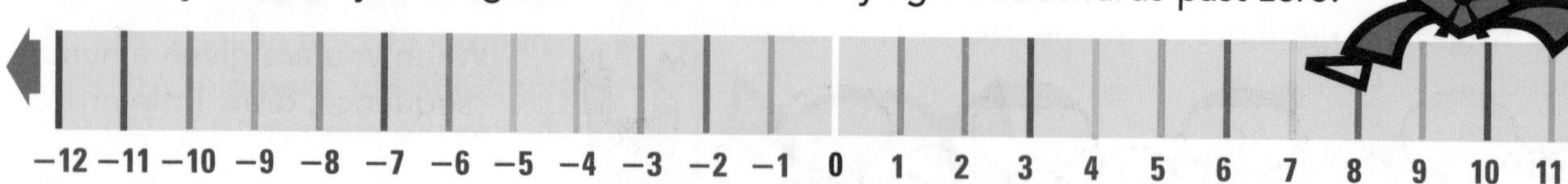

Negative numbers always have a negative sign (−) written in front of them. We don't usually bother putting the + sign in front of positive numbers... it would just be one more thing to worry about!

Temperatures on a thermometer can fall below zero.

Remember to look at the scale carefully: it's a good idea to read up or down from zero.

This shows the temperature on a cold day in Iceland... a good name for the country!

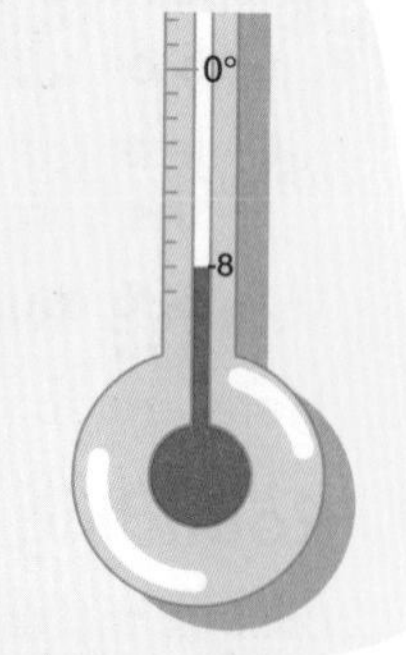

To find the difference between two temperatures, count on from the lower number.

Remember to include zero.

So the difference between

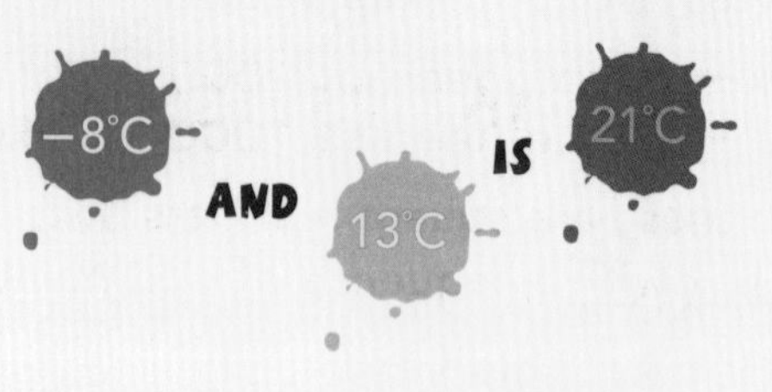

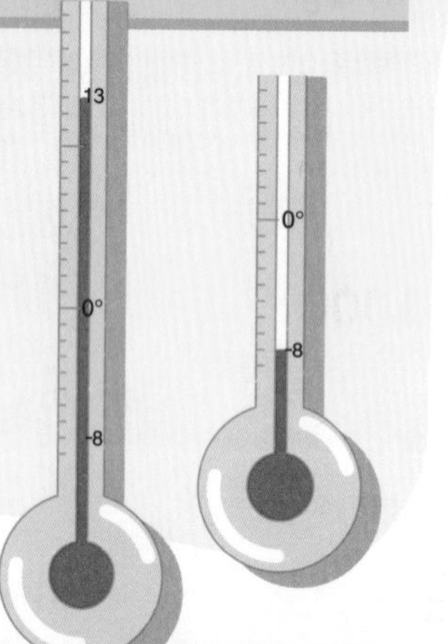

This will help...

If you need to find the difference between two negative numbers, remember that the answer will be a positive number. If your two temperatures are −3°C and −11°C the difference between them is 8°C. Sketch a number line to help you understand this.

Try these

1. Put these temperatures in order, starting with the lowest: 17°C −6°C −10°C 4°C 0°C.
2. What is the difference between 6 and −4?
3. What are the missing numbers in this sequence: −7 −5 ___ ___ 1 3 5?
4. What is 6 less than 2?

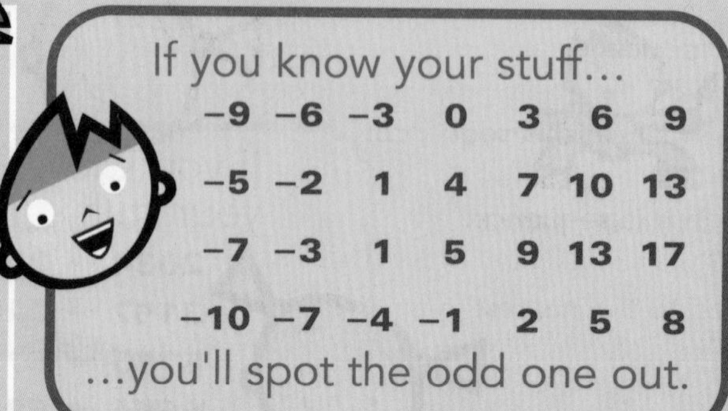

If you know your stuff...

−9	−6	−3	0	3	6	9
−5	−2	1	4	7	10	13
−7	−3	1	5	9	13	17
−10	−7	−4	−1	2	5	8

...you'll spot the odd one out.

REMEMBER

Practise going backwards and forwards on a number line...

Puzzle code

A lift stops on the ground floor of a large hotel, which has 10 floors above ground and 10 below ground. It then goes down 3 floors to −3 and then up 5 floors. If it then goes down 8 floors, where is the lift?

−8 **(R)** −5 **(A)** −6 **(Y)** −7 **(S)**

Write the letter in the grid on page 64.

 On your toes Great Britain has an area of 218 041 km^2. What is this rounded to the nearest 1000 km^2?

Number sequences

A sequence of numbers is a list of numbers with an interesting pattern.

The interesting thing is that you are often asked to find the interesting pattern!

The best thing to do is look at the **difference between the numbers.**

The **rule** here is 'add 4', so the next number is 27.

This will help...

When you are given a number sequence, draw little arrows between each number and write the differences above. This should help you work out the rule – or at least see some sort of pattern!

What's Next?

Here are some of the different types of sequence you may see.
Can you work out the next number in each sequence?

29 24 19 14 9 __

Rule: take away 5

3 5 8 12 17 __

Rule: Add an extra 1 each time

3 6 12 24 48 __

Rule: x 2 or double

Rule: these are square numbers.
Can you see a link with a sequence of odd numbers?

Try these

1. What is the next number in this sequence:
   17 23 29 35 41 __?
2. What is the rule for this sequence:
   97 88 79 70 61 52?
3. What are the missing numbers in this sequence:
   3 4 6 __ 13 18 24 __?
4. What is the 8th number in this sequence:
   7 17 27 37 47... ?

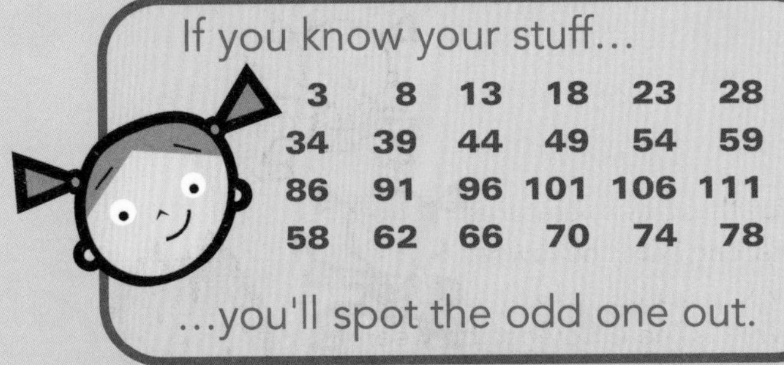

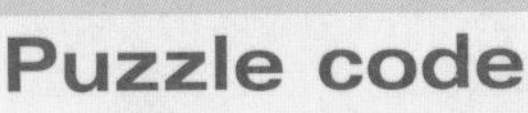

1 1 2 3 5 8 13 21 __

This is called the Fibonacci sequence. Work out the rule.
What is the next number in the sequence?

30 (S) 27 (A) 34 (O) 40 (E)

Write the letter in the grid on page 64.

In a number sequence, always look at the differences between the numbers.

1	2	3	4	5	6	
9	10	12	15	19	24	?

On your toes If the temperature goes from 11°C to a chilly –4°C, how much has it dropped?

Multiples

If you multiply a whole number by another whole number, the answer is a multiple of both numbers.

So multiples are a bit like the 'times tables' except that they go on way beyond ten times a number.

For example, the multiples:

of **3** are 3, 6, 9, 12... 36, 39, 42... etc.

of **5** are 5, 10, 15... 75, 80, 85... etc.

of **10** are 10, 20, 30... 160, 170, 180... etc.

This will help...

The tests of divisibility below are really useful if you need to work out whether a large number can be divided by 3, 4, 9 or whatever. Rather than trying a tricky division, just use the rule to work it out. For example is 35 712 divisible by 9? The digits add up to 18, so the rule says it can.

Tests of divisibility are very handy rules to test whether a number is a multiple of 2, 3, 4, 5, 6, 8, 9 or 10.

Try to learn these tests of divisibility. A whole number is a multiple of:

2 if the last digit is even.
Examples:
74, 136, 1808

3 if the sum of its digits can be divided by 3.
Examples
216 (2 + 1 + 6 = 9), 3741 (3 + 7 + 4 + 1 = 15)

4 if the last two digits together can be divided by 4.
Examples: 132, 508, 6212

5 if the last digit is 0 or 5.
Examples:
910, 1025, 3660

6 if it is even and the sum of its digits can be divided by 3.
Examples: 474 (4 + 7 + 4 = 15), 4152 (4 + 1 + 5 + 2 = 12)

8 if half of it can be divided by 4.
Examples:
664, 352, 792

9 if the sum of its digits can be divided by 9.
Examples: 351 (3 + 5 + 1 = 9), 657 (6 + 5 + 7 = 18)

10 if the last digit is 0.
Examples:
230, 690, 1400

Try these

1 What is the next multiple of 4 after 60?
2 Is 327 a multiple of 6?
3 Which two multiples of 3 are between 140 and 145?
4 Is 35 716 divisible by 4?

If you know your stuff...

309

27 51

136

150

...you'll spot the odd one out.

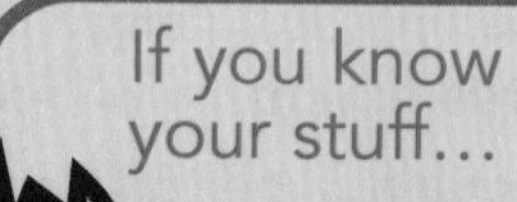

Make sure you know your multiplication patterns.

Puzzle code

Which of these numbers is a multiple of both 3 and 4?

94 **(R)** 160 **(B)** 306 **(L)** 132 **(U)** *Write the letter in the grid on page 64.*

 On your toes What is the next number in this sequence? 34 31 28 25 22 ☐

Factors

A factor of a whole number is any whole number that divides exactly into it.

This sounds a bit complicated, so look at this example:

Factors of 24 → 1, 2, 3, 4, 6, 8, 12, 24 →
8 factors that divide exactly into 24.

It is a good idea to write factors in pairs.

This makes it easier to see if you've included them all:

So factors of 30 → (1, 30) (2, 15) (3, 10) (5, 6) → 8

You can see from this brick wall that the 30 single bricks on the bottom (30, 1) come to the same as the 15 double blocks above (15, 2) and so on up to the 5 large blocks at the top (5, 6).

1, 2, 3 and 6 are **common factors** of 18 and 30: that means they're factors of both these numbers. The **highest common factor** of 18 and 30 is 6. So 6 is the largest number that will divide exactly into both 18 and 30.

Did you notice that 1 and the number itself are always factors?

If a number has only these two factors, it is called a **prime number**. The factors of 13 are (1, 13), so 13 is a prime number.

This will help...

Numbers always have an even number of factors, unless they are square numbers. The factors of square numbers can be written as pairs, but look at these:

Factors of 16 → (1, 16) (2, 8) (4, 4) → 5 factors

Factors of 25 → (1, 25) (5, 5) → 3 factors

1 is not a prime number as it only has one factor: 1

Try these

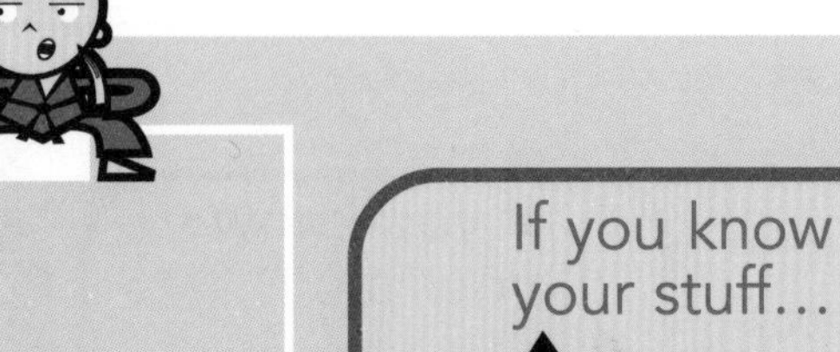

1 List the factors of 20.
2 Is 27 a prime number?
3 Is 9 a factor of 45?
4 What is the highest common factor of 21 and 28?

Puzzle code

Which of these numbers is a factor of both 32 and 48?

6 (R) 3 (D) 12 (M) 8 (H)

Write the letter in the grid on page 64.

REMEMBER

Factors are all the numbers that divide exactly into another number.

On your toes Which two multiples of 4 are between 90 and 99?

Special numbers

Revise wise

Multiples, factors and prime numbers are special, but there are others that like to think they're pretty cool.

Square roots are the opposite of square numbers.

To find the square root of 36, find a number which multiplies by itself to make 36.

$6 \times 6 = 36$

When a number is multiplied by itself, it makes a square number.

$1 \times 1 = 1$ $2 \times 2 = 4$ $3 \times 3 = 9$

$4 \times 4 = 16$ $5 \times 5 = 25$ $6 \times 6 = 36$

So 1, 4, 9, 16, 25 and 36 are square numbers.

Another way of writing 3×3 is with a small ^{2}.

So 3×3 is 3^2, which means 'three squared'.

$3^2 = 9$ $7^2 = 49$ $10^2 = 100$

Odds and evens.

These are well known special numbers. Just remember:

- even numbers end in 0, 2, 4, 6 and 8
- odd numbers end in 1, 3, 5, 7 and 9.

Triangular numbers make triangular pattern.

Here are the first six triangular numbers:

1 3 6 10 15 21

$0 + 1 = 1$

$1 + 2 = 3$

$1 + 2 + 3 = 6$

$1 + 2 + 3 + 4 = 10$

$1 + 2 + 3 + 4 + 5 = 15$

$1 + 2 + 3 + 4 + 5 + 6 = 21$

This will help...

Square numbers can be shown as a pattern of squares.

Triangular numbers can be shown as a pattern of triangles.

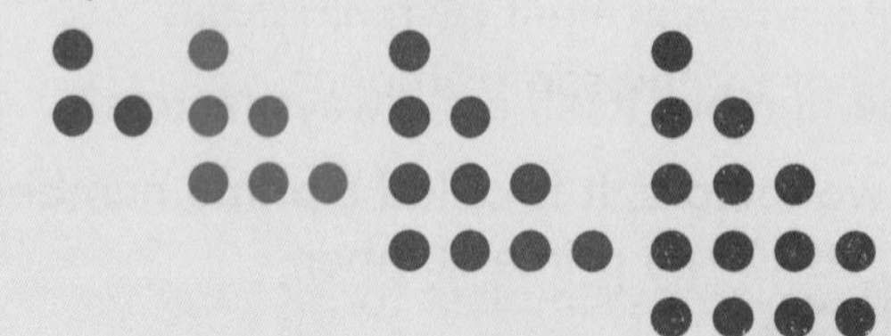

If you add up consecutive triangular numbers, you'll see a link between square and triangular numbers.

Try these

1 Which is the next square number after 100?
2 What is 8^2?
3 Is 45 a triangular number?
4 $\sqrt{81} =$ ___

If you know your stuff...

49 81

15 25

...you'll spot the odd one out.

Puzzle code

Which number between 20 and 40 is both a triangular number and a square number?

36 (A) 25 (I) 21 (E) 35 (O)

Write the letter in the grid on page 64.

REMEMBER

Square numbers

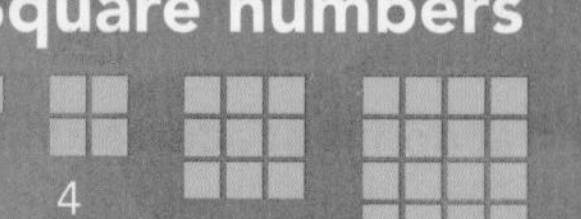

1 4 9 16 25 *and so*

Triangular numbers

1 3 6 10 *and*

 On your toes What are the factors of 36?

Fractions

A fraction is a certain number of equal parts of a whole.

$\frac{3}{4}$ means 3 equal parts out of 4.

When you write a fraction it has two numbers:

3	→	numerator	The numerator tells you how many of these equal parts you are using.
4	→	denominator	The denominator shows you the number of equal parts.

$\frac{1}{6}$ eaten

$\frac{2}{6}$ eaten

$\frac{3}{6}$ eaten

$\frac{4}{6}$ eaten

$\frac{5}{6}$ eaten

$\frac{6}{6}$ eaten

Remember that $\frac{2}{2}$, $\frac{3}{3}$, $\frac{4}{4}$, $\frac{5}{5}$, etc. are all the same as one whole.

Equivalent fractions are worth the same, even though they may look different.

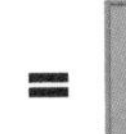

$\frac{3}{5} = \frac{6}{10} = \frac{9}{15}$

Have another look at the pizza. Which fractions are equivalent to $\frac{2}{6}$, $\frac{3}{6}$ and $\frac{4}{6}$?

You can change a fraction into an equivalent by multiplying the numerator and denominator by the same amount:

$$\frac{2 \times 3}{3 \times 3} = \frac{6}{9}$$

You can cancel the fraction down to its simplest form by dividing in the same way:

$$\frac{16 \div 4}{20 \div 4} = \frac{4}{5}$$

This will help...

If you need to work out if two fractions are equivalent, start by looking at the denominators (the bottom numbers). If one divides into the other, then check the top numbers to see if they divide in the same way. If they do, the fractions are equivalent.

Try these

1 What fraction is shaded?

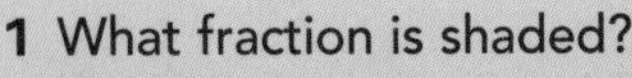

2 Draw a square. Shade it to show $\frac{7}{8}$.

3 Complete this $\frac{3}{4} = \frac{}{20}$

4 What is $\frac{12}{30}$ in its simplest form?

If you know your stuff...

$\frac{1}{3}$ $\frac{5}{15}$ $\frac{10}{30}$ $\frac{7}{24}$ $\frac{3}{9}$

...you'll spot the odd one out.

The bricks in this wall show equivalent fractions:

Puzzle code

Write the letter in the grid on page 64.

Which fraction is equivalent to $\frac{5}{6}$? $\frac{12}{42}$ (D) $\frac{6}{9}$ (L) $\frac{20}{24}$ (V) $\frac{30}{42}$ (R)

On your toes Which number between 100 and 200 is a square number and a multiple of 9?

Comparing fractions

Putting fractions in order of size is easy if all the denominators are the same, but a lot trickier if the denominators are different.

If a set of fractions all have the same denominator, then you just need to put the numerators in order.

An example using same denominators

Put these in order, starting with the smallest: $\frac{3}{10}, \frac{7}{10}, \frac{9}{10}, \frac{1}{10}$

Check the numerators and put them in order: $\frac{1}{10}, \frac{3}{10}, \frac{7}{10}, \frac{9}{10}$

If a set of fractions has different denominators, find equivalent fractions with the same denominator.

This is called finding the common denominator. It makes fractions much easier to compare.

Put these in order, starting with the smallest: $\frac{3}{4}, \frac{2}{3}, \frac{5}{6}, \frac{1}{2}$

Looking at the denominators and find a number that they can all be multiplied to make. This is the **common denominator**. All the denominators can be multiplied to make 12, so change them all to twelfths:

$\frac{3}{4} = \frac{3 \times 3}{4 \times 3} = \frac{9}{12}$ $\quad \frac{2}{3} = \frac{2 \times 4}{3 \times 4} = \frac{8}{12}$

$\frac{5}{6} = \frac{5 \times 2}{6 \times 2} = \frac{10}{12}$ $\quad \frac{1}{2} = \frac{1 \times 6}{2 \times 6} = \frac{6}{12}$

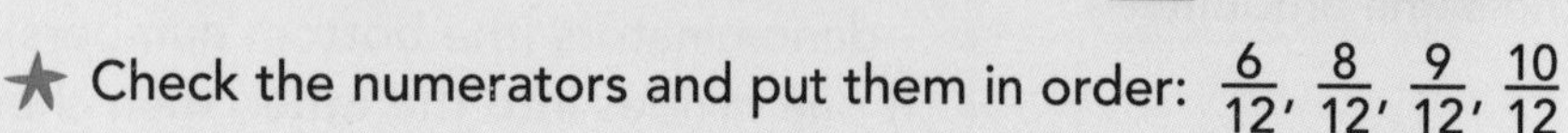

★ Check the numerators and put them in order: $\frac{6}{12}, \frac{8}{12}, \frac{9}{12}, \frac{10}{12}$

★ Change the fractions back for your answer: $\frac{1}{2}, \frac{2}{3}, \frac{3}{4}, \frac{5}{6}$

This will help...

Making common denominators is one way of comparing fractions.
Here are two other methods of comparing fractions.
Which is bigger, $\frac{4}{5}$ or $\frac{2}{3}$?

Make an equivalence strip for each fraction.

Make two strips the same length, then divide them and shade sections to show the fractions.

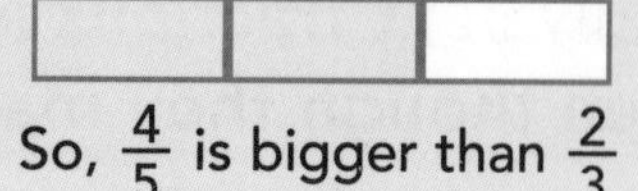

So, $\frac{4}{5}$ is bigger than $\frac{2}{3}$

Fractions → decimals

$\frac{4}{5} = 0.8$ $\quad \frac{2}{3} = 0.666...$

0.8 is bigger than 0.666..., so $\frac{4}{5}$ is bigger than $\frac{2}{3}$.

Compare fractions using common denominators

$\frac{5}{6} \rightarrow \frac{10}{12}$, $\frac{2}{3} \rightarrow \frac{8}{12}$

$\frac{10}{12} > \frac{8}{12}$

Try these

1 Write these fractions in order, starting with the largest: $\frac{7}{12}, \frac{3}{12}, \frac{11}{12}, \frac{1}{12}$

2 Which is greater, $\frac{2}{5}$ or $\frac{3}{10}$?

3 Write these in order, starting with the smallest: $\frac{3}{4}, \frac{3}{8}, \frac{1}{4}, \frac{5}{8}$

4 Is $\frac{7}{15}$ greater or less than $\frac{1}{2}$?

Puzzle code

Which is the missing fraction? $\frac{2}{3} >$ __ $> \frac{1}{2}$ $\quad \frac{2}{5}$ **(R)** $\quad \frac{1}{4}$ **(L)** $\quad \frac{3}{5}$ **(E)** $\quad \frac{3}{4}$ **(T)**

Write the letter in the grid on page 64.

 On your toes What is $\frac{15}{20}$ as a fraction reduced to its simplest form?

Fractions of quantities

If you want to find fractions of shapes or amounts, the **numerator** and **denominator** are the key players again.players again.

numerator → 2
3 ← denominator

Finding $\frac{1}{2}$ or $\frac{1}{3}$ or $\frac{1}{4}$ or $\frac{1}{8}$ ... of a shape or amount is the same as dividing by the denominator.

The numerator is 1 so it's simple.

$\frac{1}{5}$ of this choccy bar is 1 piece:

When the numerator is more than 1 you divide by the denominator then multiply by the numerator.

$\frac{3}{5}$ of this choccy bar:

Alex buys 45 doughnuts. He eats one-fifth of them before he gets home. How many does he eat?

$\frac{1}{5}$ of 45 = 45 ÷ 5 = 9

If you're still struggling with this, look at it another way. You could change the fractions to decimals of amounts. The word 'of' means 'multiplied by'.

So, to find $\frac{3}{10}$ of 80, change $\frac{3}{10}$ to 0.3

so 0.3 × 80 =

24

Alex gives $\frac{3}{5}$ of his 45 doughnuts to his sister as he is on a diet. How many does she eat?

$\frac{1}{5}$ of 45 = 9

$\frac{3}{5}$ of 45 = 9 × 3 = 27

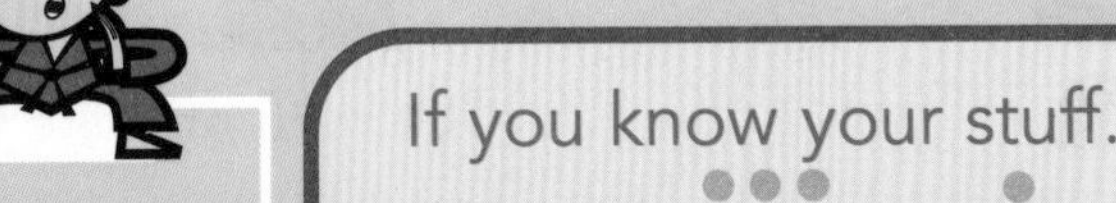

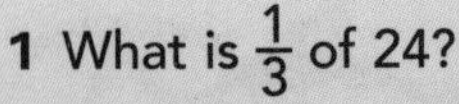

1 What is $\frac{1}{3}$ of 24?

2 What is $\frac{3}{4}$ of 20?

3 A bottle holds 300 ml of lemonade. If $\frac{3}{5}$ is drunk, how much is left?

4 What is $\frac{3}{10}$ of £4.50?

Divide by the bottom

and then multiply by the top.

Puzzle code

Huma has 35 CDs and decides to give $\frac{2}{5}$ of her CD collection to her mother. How many is she left with?

14 (Y) 21 (F) 12 (R) 25 (C)

Write the letter in the grid on page 64.

On your toes Which fraction is bigger, $\frac{3}{4}$ or $\frac{7}{10}$?

Ratio and proportion

Ratio and proportion are similar ideas, so they can easily get confused.

They are quite different though, so read this carefully.

Finding the proportion of an amount

This is the same as finding the fraction of the whole amount.

Unknown to man, the only intelligent life-forms on the moon are Lunar-tics. They can be recognised by their unusual markings.

What proportion (or fraction) of their spots are red?

There are 6 spots altogether, 2 of them are red, so $\frac{1}{3}$ of the spots are red.

This means that the proportion of red spots is 1 in every 3, or $\frac{1}{3}$.

Ratio compares one part or amount with another.

So don't worry about the total, just look at one amount compared with another. If you look back at the spots on the Lunar-tics they are in the ratio of 2 red spots to every 4 yellow, which is 2:4 or 1:2.

Lunar-tics' favourite food is meatballs and peas (all their food is spherical) in the ratio of 1:4.

The ratio stays the same for different amounts:

meatballs	peas
1	4
2	8
3	12
4	16

If they had 36 peas, how many meatballs would they have?

This will help...

Think about a tile pattern to help you understand ratio.

The pattern starts with a white tile then two black tiles.
The ratio of white to black tiles is 1 to every 2, or 1:2
If the pattern went on and on the ratio would stay the same

The ratio of white to black tiles is still 1:2

Try these

1 Tom makes a drink in the ratio of 2 lemons to every 3 oranges. If he uses 8 lemons, how many oranges will he need?

2 What proportion of these glasses are full?

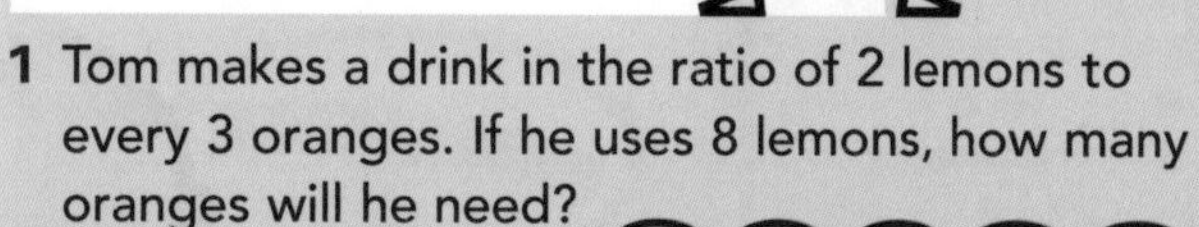

3 There are 5 toffees to every 2 soft-centres in a box of 21 chocolates. How many soft-centres are there in the box?

4 What is the ratio of buns with pink icing to buns with white icing?

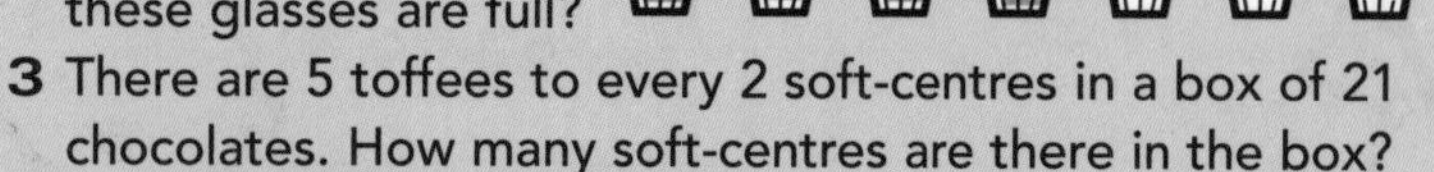

Puzzle code

At the swimming club there are 3 boys for every 4 girls. There are 35 children at the club. How many boys are there?

18 **(R)** 21 **(L)** 15 **(I)** 20 **(E)** *Write the letter in the grid on page 64.*

REMEMBER

Proportion: a fraction of the whole amount.

Of the stars, 1 in every 4 or $\frac{1}{4}$ are yellow.

Ratio: compares quantities.

The ratio of yellow to blue is 1 to every 3 or 1:3

 On your toes 75 tulip bulbs are planted. $\frac{3}{5}$ of the flowers are red and the rest are yellow. How many are red?

Decimal notation

In a decimal number, the decimal point shows where the whole number ends and the decimal fraction begins.

tens	ones	.	tenths	hundredths	thousandths
3	4	.	8	2	
	7	.	1	5	2
	0	.	6	9	
1	9	.	4	3	7

1 9 . 4 3 7

- tens (1 ten)
- ones (9 ones)
- tenths ($\frac{4}{10}$)
- hundredths ($\frac{3}{100}$)
- thousandths ($\frac{7}{1000}$)

This will help...

You can break up a decimal number to see each part clearly:

$$38.437 = 30 + 8 + \frac{4}{10} + \frac{3}{100} + \frac{7}{1000}$$

0 10 20 30 40 50 60 70 80 90 100 cm

Try to picture one metre in your head.

One-tenth is 10 cm.

One-hundredth is 1 cm.

One-thousandth is 1 mm.

Putting a zero on the end of a decimal doesn't change the number. 1.8 is the same as 1.80 and 1.800

Try these

1. What is $\frac{3}{10}$ as a decimal?
2. What is $\frac{4}{100}$ as a decimal?
3. How many hundredths are there in the number 6.078?
4. Which is larger, 7.195 or 7.29?

If you know your stuff...

17.30

17.3

17.300

17.03

...you'll spot the odd one out.

$0.1 \rightarrow \frac{1}{10}$

$0.01 \rightarrow \frac{1}{100}$

$0.001 \rightarrow \frac{1}{1000}$

Puzzle code

What is this number? $7 + \frac{3}{10} + \frac{5}{100} + \frac{9}{1000}$

7.3159 **(R)** 73.59 **(L)** 7.309 **(V)** 7.359 **(N)**

Write the letter in the grid on page 64.

On your toes You need 1 tin of *Polar* paint to 4 tins of *Mint*. For 3 tins of *Polar*, how many tins of *Mint*?

Decimal places

Revise wise

To multiply and divide decimals by 10 or 100, follow the same simple rules as for whole numbers:

Multiply by 10

Move the digits **one place** to the left.

8 . 2 5 × 10 =

8 2 . 5

Divide by 10

Move the digits **one place** to the right.

6 3 . 7 ÷ 10 =

6 . 3 7

Multiply by 100

Move the digits **two places** to the left.

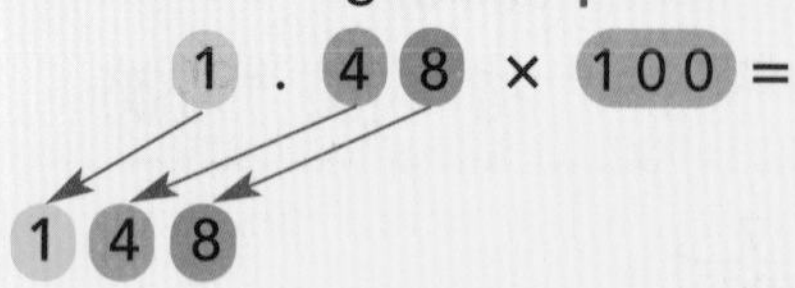

Divide by 100

Move the digits **two places** to the right.

3 9 . 6 ÷ 100 =

0 . 3 9 6

Don't forget the different values of each part of a decimal number.

A long-haired hippo (the hippy-pottomus) is 3.814 m long, including his ponytail.

← 3.814m →

ones (3 ones)

tenths ($\frac{8}{10}$)

hundredths ($\frac{1}{100}$)

thousandths ($\frac{4}{1000}$)

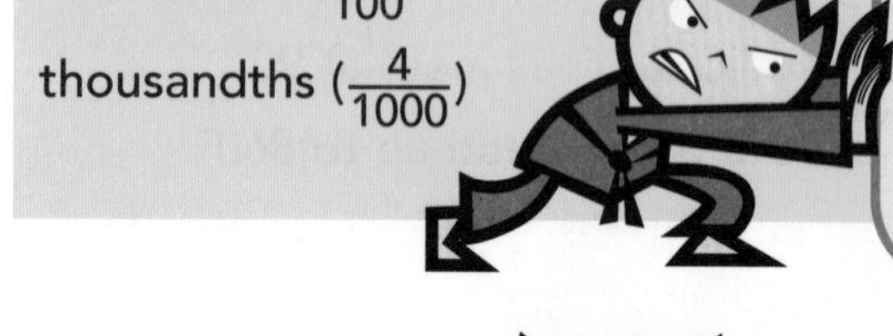

This will help...

Make a set of digit cards and a decimal point card. Now make a number, like 3.16. Follow these steps, remembering to move the digits left and right and not the decimal point:

3.16 → × 10 → × 10 → ÷ 100 → ÷ 10 → × 1000 → ÷ 100 → 3.16

Try it with different starting numbers.

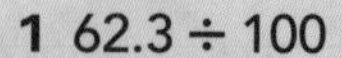

Try these

1 62.3 ÷ 100

2 Which number is 10 times larger than 0.08?

3 4.08 × ___ = 408

4 ___ ÷ 10 = 0.36

If you know your stuff...

3.1 → 0.31
1.8 → 0.18
0.6 → 0.06
2.7 → 0.72

...you'll spot the odd one out.

Multiplying by 10 or 100 moves the digits

← to the left.

Dividing by 10 or 100 moves the digits

to the right. →

Puzzle code

The web of a common garden spider contains as much as 30 m of silk, yet the web's mass is only 0.05 g. If 100 spiders build webs in a garden, what is the total web mass?

0.5 g **(D)**   5 g **(I)**   500 g **(T)**   0.005 g **(A)**

Write the letter in the grid on page 64.

 On your toes How many hundredths are there in 352.37?

Ordering decimals

Comparing the size of decimals can be tricky, particularly when there are different numbers of digits.

When you need to put decimals in order it is helpful to write them under each other, lining up the decimal point.

These are the results of a snail race, with distances travelled in 1 year.

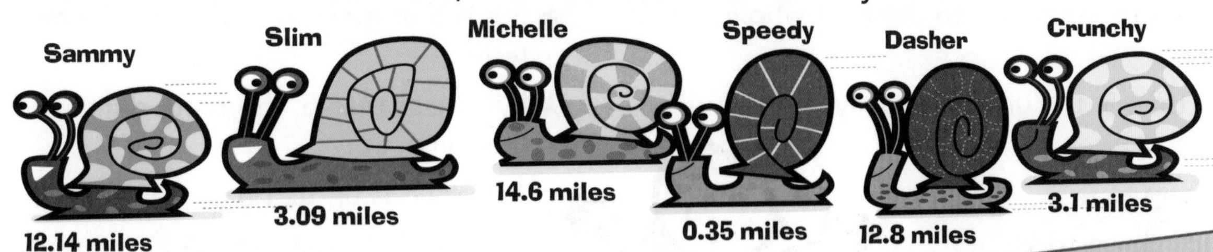

Write the distances under each other:

Remember to line up the decimal points

12.74
3.09
14.6
0.35
12.8
3.1

Now put them in order:

Compare the tens first, then the units, tenths and hundredths:

14.6
12.8
12.74
3.1
3.09
0.35

< means is less than
For example 2.65 < 2.7
2.65 is less than 2.7

> means is greater than
For example 1.6 > 1.31
1.6 is greater than 1.31

This will help...

When you have a list of decimal numbers, it can be easier to compare them if you put zeros on the end, so that they all have the same number of digits.

For example:
3.01, 3.6, 3.9, 3.1, 3.92
are easier to compare if you write them as
3.01, 3.60, 3.90, 3.10, 3.92

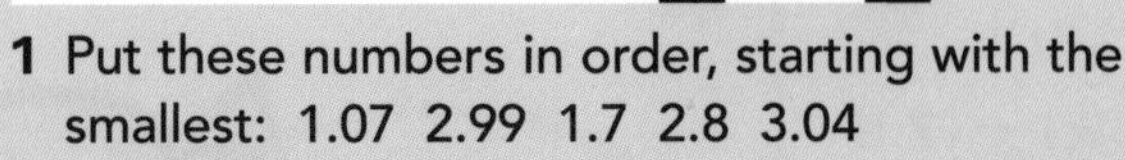

1 Put these numbers in order, starting with the smallest: 1.07 2.99 1.7 2.8 3.04
2 Which is the larger number, 9.2 or 9.18?
3 Which sign is missing, < or >?
16.03 □ 16.3
4 Give three numbers that could go in the box:
1.71 > □ > 1.6

If you know your stuff...

2.6 > 2.16

3.55 < 3.58

1.29 > 1.3

0.7 < 0.82

...you'll spot the odd one out.

When you're comparing decimals, line up the decimal points.

Puzzle code

These are the wingspans of some pretty big birds:

trumpeter swan	marabou stork	black vulture	albatross
3.39 m	3.97 m	3.09 m	3.7 m

Which is the missing bird? marabou stork > ? > trumpeter swan

trumpeter swan **(T)** black vulture **(P)** albatross **(S)** marabou stork **(R)**

Write the letter in the grid on page 64.

On your toes Which number is ten times smaller than 13.8?

Rounding decimals

We round decimals for the same reason as we round large numbers – it makes them easier to work with. We usually round decimals to the nearest whole number or tenth.

Rounding to the nearest whole number

- ★ Look at the **tenths** digit.
- ★ If it is 5 or more, round up to the next whole number.
- ★ If it is less than 5, the units digit stays the same. So:

  3.5 rounds up to 4

  9.46 rounds down to 9

Rounding to the nearest tenth

- ★ Look at the **hundredths** digit.
- ★ If it is 5 or more, round up to the next tenth.
- ★ If it is less than 5, the tenth digit stays the same. So:

  1.76 rounds up to 1.8

  2.918 rounds down to 2.9

This will help...

If you're not sure which way to round a decimal, draw a quick number line with whole numbers on either side of your number. So to round 6.37, draw a line from 6 to 7 and mark off the tenths. Draw an arrow to show 6.37 and you can see it is nearer to 6.

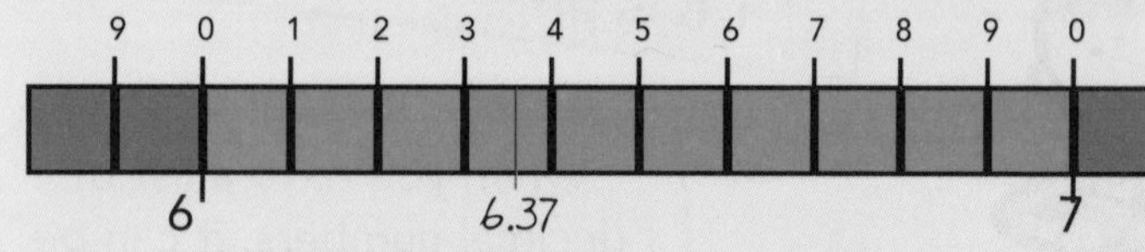

Rounding to the nearest tenth is sometimes called rounding to one decimal place.

Tom collects loose change in a bottle. Every year he empties the bottle and spends the money on a slap-up meal at the local pie shop. Over the last 4 years he has collected the following amounts:

How much has he collected in total?

To the nearest whole number → £6 + £7 + £6 + £8 = £27

To the nearest tenth → £5.80 + £6.90 + £6.30 + £8.30 = £27.30

≈ means is approximately equal to

£5.76 + £6.92 + £6.34 + £8.29 ≈ £27

Try these

1. What is 34.67 kg rounded to the nearest kilogram?
2. What is £138.45 rounded to the nearest 10 pence?
3. 7.84 × 3.19 ≈ ___
4. What is the approximate difference between 12.39 and 7.84?

If you know your stuff...

7.91 → 7.9

8.472 → 8.5

16.82 → 16.8

3.641 → 3.7

...you'll spot the odd one out.

To round to the nearest whole number → look at the tenth.

To round to the nearest tenth → look at the hundredth.

Puzzle code

On a fishing trip, Dan somehow manages to catch two sharks – one weighing 1.873 tonnes and the other weighing 5.329 tonnes. What is the approximate difference between these weights?

7.1 tonnes **(T)** 3.4 tonnes **(H)**

4.3 tonnes **(S)** 5.1 tonnes **(A)**

Write the letter in the grid on page 64.

 On your toes What is the missing number? 9.39 < ___ < 9.41

Decimals and fractions

In a way, fractions and decimals are the same thing – parts of a whole number.

They are just written differently. It is useful to be able to change fractions to decimals and the other way round.

Before we go any further, here are some that you just need to know:

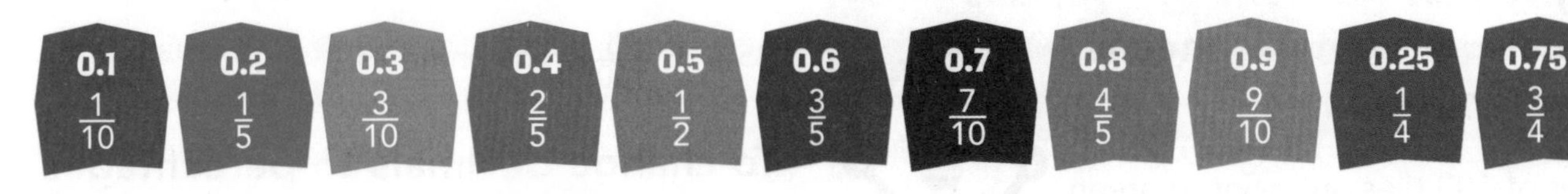

$\frac{1}{3}$ is 0.3333... and $\frac{2}{3}$ is 0.6666... The decimals are recurring, that means they go on and on.

Cover each one up with your finger and see if you know the equivalent decimal or fraction.

Converting decimals to fractions

- Try to learn all the tenths in the table above.
- If it is a hundredths decimal, like 0.64, then write it as a fraction out of 100: $\frac{64}{100}$.

  Then simplify this by dividing:

  $$\frac{64}{100}\ (\div 4) = \frac{16}{25}$$

- If it is a thousandths decimal, like 0.185, then write it as a fraction out of 1000: $\frac{185}{1000}$.

  Then simplify this by dividing:

  $$\frac{185}{1000}\ (\div 5) = \frac{37}{200}$$

Converting fractions to decimals

- The line in a fraction means 'divided by'. So write it as a division:

$\frac{3}{8} = 3 \div 8 = 0.375$

Put in some extra zeros after the decimal point to help with the written calculation.

$$8\overline{)3.000}\ = 0.375$$

If you can use a calculator, this becomes really simple.

This will help...

Number lines can come in handy again here. Draw a number line from 0–1 and mark on the tenths. You can then show different fractions or decimals on the line and convert them. Look at these:

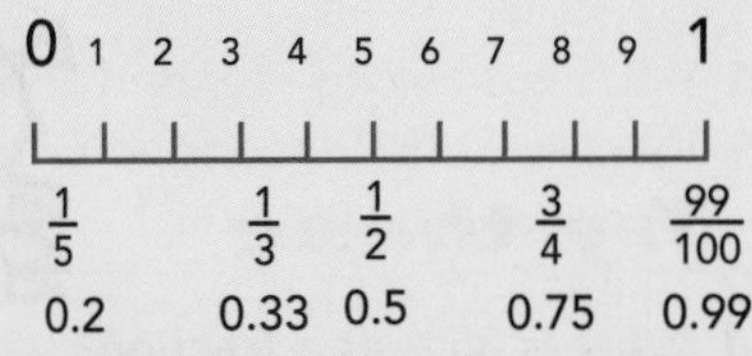

When you convert a fraction to a decimal it will always be less than 1.

Try these

1 What is 0.8 as a fraction?

2 What is $\frac{7}{100}$ as a decimal?

3 Which is greater, 0.3 or $\frac{1}{3}$?

4 Which fraction is the same as 0.84?

If you know your stuff...

0.4 → $\frac{2}{5}$

0.4 → $\frac{1}{2}$

0.4 → $\frac{7}{10}$

0.4 → $\frac{1}{3}$

...you'll spot the odd one out.

Divide the top by the bottom to change a fraction into a decimal.

$\frac{3}{4} = 3 \div 4 = 0.75$

Puzzle code

What is 0.875 as a fraction in its simplest form?

$\frac{17}{40}$ **(I)** $\frac{7}{9}$ **(D)** $\frac{17}{25}$ **(T)** $\frac{7}{8}$ **(E)**

Write the letter in the grid on page 64.

On your toes What is 28.364 litres rounded to the nearest tenth of a litre?

Percentages

Revise wise

Percentages are used a lot in everyday life, so they must be simple to use!

And they are...

They're just fractions of 100, this is what per cent (%) means – 'in every 100'.

35 out of 100 tiles are painted green.

So 35% of the wall is green.
What percentage has the painter still got to paint?

To change fractions to percentages

make them out of 100:

15 out of the 25 tiles are painted red, which is $\frac{15}{25}$.

Work out an equivalent fraction with the denominator 100.

$\frac{15}{25} \rightarrow (\times 4) \rightarrow \frac{60}{100} = 60\%$

To change percentages to fractions

write the percentage as a fraction out of 100 and then simplify:

80% or $\frac{80}{100}$ is the same as $\frac{4}{5}$

25% or $\frac{25}{100}$ is the same as $\frac{4}{5}$

To change decimals to percentages

multiply the decimal by 100:

0.8 is the same as 80%

0.45 is the same as 45%

To change percentages to decimals

divide the percentage by 100:

40% is the same as 0.4

95% is the same as 0.95

When you change a percentage to a decimal, remember that it will always be less than 1 if the percentage is less than 100%.

This will help...

Another good way of changing a fraction to a percentage is to change it to a decimal and then multiply by 100. A calculator is useful for this!

Example:
What percentage of a sticker book is completed if you have 78 out of 150 stickers?

$\frac{78}{150}$ is 0.52, which is the same as 52%.

Try these

1 What is 35% as a fraction?

2 What is $\frac{9}{10}$ as a percentage?

3 Anna scored $\frac{18}{20}$ in a tables test.
What percentage did she score?

4 Which is greater, 60% or $\frac{17}{25}$?

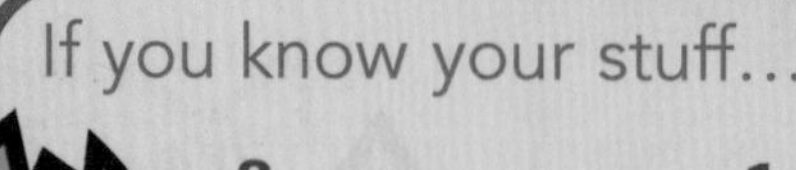

$\frac{2}{5}$ **40%** **0.4** $\frac{1}{4}$

...you'll spot the odd one out.

Percentages are fractions out of 100:

$\frac{3}{4} = \frac{75}{100} = 0.75 = 75\%$

Puzzle code

Which one of these is the highest percentage?

20 out of 25 **(D)** 15 out of 20 **(N)**
7 out of 10 **(R)** 30 out of 50 **(T)**

Write the letter in the grid on page 64.

 On your toes Which is smaller, 0.04 or $\frac{1}{20}$?

Percentages of amounts

Once you understand what percentages are, you need to be able to use them.

Most questions about percentages ask you to find percentages of amounts. This is just the same as using fractions.

There are 60 sheep in a field. 20% of them escape by jumping over the fence while the farmer is counting them in his sleep.

How many sheep escape?

You are trying to find 20% of 60.

With this type of question, the word 'of' means multiply.

Try these three methods:

Change to a fraction

and work it out:

$\frac{20}{100} \times 60 = \frac{1200}{100} = 12$

Change to a decimal

and work it out: 0.2 3 60 5 12

Use 10%

to work it out. Just divide by 10: 10% of 60 is 6.

So, 20% of 60 is double that: 12

This will help...

Using 10% and 1% is a good way of working out percentages quickly:

10% is the same as $\frac{1}{10}$

10% of £24 = £2.40

5% → half 10% → £1.20
20% → double 10% → £4.80
30% → 3 × 10% → £7.20

1% is the same as $\frac{1}{100}$

1% of £80 = 80p

2% → double 1% → £1.60
3% → 3 × 1% → £2.40

Sale prices in shops often use percentages.

Just remember the two steps to work out the sale price:

Step 1: work out the amount you save.

30% of £40 is £12.

Step 2: take away this amount from the price.

£40 take away £12 is £28.

So the sale price is £28 (still too much!).

Try these

1. What is 5% of £20?
2. What is 40% of 500?
3. A scarf is reduced in a sale by 60%. If it was originally £8, what is the sale price?
4. Mel has 80 sausages in her freezer. She used 15% for a barbecue. How many has she got left?

Use 10% to work out other percentages.

Puzzle code

There are 120 cars for sale in a car supermarket.
In one week, 25% are sold. How many cars are still for sale?

80 (R) 40 (N) 30 (L) 90 (T)

Write the letter in the grid on page 64.

On your toes What is $\frac{3}{5}$ as a percentage?

Number facts

There are certain number facts that you just need to know.

They are like the nuts and bolts that hold everything else together. Knowing your addition and subtraction bonds or tables will certainly make dealing with mental calculations a lot more enjoyable!

Use these two grids to learn key facts.

Addition and subtraction

+	1	2	3	4	5	6	7	8	9	10
1	2	3	4	5	6	7	8	9	10	11
2	3	4	5	6	7	8	9	10	11	12
3	4	5	6	7	8	9	10	11	12	13
4	5	6	7	8	9	10	11	12	13	14
5	6	7	8	9	10	11	12	13	14	15
6	7	8	9	10	11	12	13	14	15	16
7	8	9	10	11	12	13	14	15	16	17
8	9	10	11	12	13	14	15	16	17	18
9	10	11	12	13	14	15	16	17	18	19
10	11	12	13	14	15	16	17	18	19	20

Multiplication and division

×	1	2	3	4	5	6	7	8	9	10
1	1	2	3	4	5	6	7	8	9	10
2	2	4	6	8	10	12	14	16	18	20
3	3	6	9	12	15	18	21	24	27	30
4	4	8	12	16	20	24	28	32	36	40
5	5	10	15	20	25	30	35	40	45	50
6	6	12	18	24	30	36	42	48	54	60
7	7	14	21	28	35	42	49	56	63	70
8	8	16	24	32	40	48	56	64	72	80
9	9	18	27	36	45	54	63	72	81	90
10	10	20	30	40	50	60	70	80	90	100

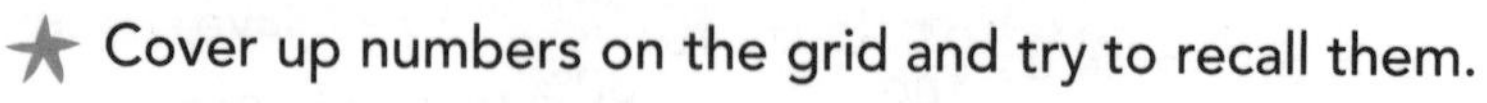

- ★ Cover up numbers on the grid and try to recall them.
- ★ Ask someone to read out pairs of numbers around the edge – answer as quickly as possible.
- ★ Ask someone to read a number within the grid – give pairs of outside numbers as quickly as possible.
- ★ Colour in any **sums** or **products** on each grid that you find tricky.

This will help...

Addition and subtraction are linked. If you know one fact, you can quickly work out three others:

$7 + 6 = 13$ $13 - 7 = 6$
$6 + 7 = 13$ $13 - 6 = 7$

Multiplication and division are linked in the same way. Use one fact to help recall the others:

$4 \times 7 = 28$ $28 \div 4 = 7$
$7 \times 4 = 28$ $28 \div 7 = 4$

Try these

Answer these as quickly as possible:

1 3×6 9×4 7×7 8×6
2 $8 + 7$ $6 + 5$ $9 + 4$ $6 + 8$
3 $13 - 6$ $11 - 7$ $18 - 9$ $17 - 10$
4 $45 \div 9$ $28 \div 4$ $42 \div 6$ $27 \div 3$

Puzzle code

What is the difference between these two products: 7×9 and 4×8?

31 **(H)** 63 **(R)** 32 **(A)** 95 **(E)**

Write the letter in the grid on page 64.

If you know your stuff...

3×3
$15 - 7$
$5 + 4$
$72 \div 8$

...you'll spot the odd one out.

- + → add, sum, total
- − → difference, subtract, take away
- × → product, times, multiply
- ÷ → divide, share, quotient

 On your toes Roger goes shopping with £90. He spends 5% on his lunch. How much has he got left?

Mental addition

When you add numbers in your head, the first thing you should do is **look at the numbers** to work out the **best method** to use. There is no set method – choose the one that works for you and the one that works best for the numbers you are adding.

Breaking up the smaller number is a good way of adding:

68 + 54 is the same as
68 + 50 + 4 → 118 + 4 → 122

Breaking up both numbers could work:

56 + 85 is the same as
(50 + 80) + (6 + 5) → 130 + 11 → 141

This will help...

Numbers can be added in any order:

43 + 88 = 88+43

37 +95 = 95 +37

Change the order so that you hold the largest number in your head and add on the smaller number.

Rounding numbers is useful if the units digit is 8 or 9:

74 + 49 is the same as
74 + (50 – 1) → 124 – 1 → 123

Use number facts and place value if you are adding big numbers or decimals:

600 + 900 → if you know that 6 + 9 is 15, then this is 100 times bigger → 1500

7.8 + 6.6 → 7 + 6 is 13 and 0.8 + 0.6 is 1.4 → 13 + 1.4 → 14.4

Try these

1 What is the sum of 47 and 76?
2 Toni's ice cream van sells 38 cornets in the morning and 53 in the afternoon. How many cornets are sold altogether?
3 What is 57 + 69?
4 1200 + 950 =

Puzzle code

What is the total of these three numbers:

8.4 9.6 3.7

20.7 **(O)** 22.3 **(R)** 22.1 **(A)** 21.7 **(I)** *Write the letter in the grid on page 64.*

If you know your stuff...

38 + 27

42 + 23

29 + 46

34 + 31

...you'll spot the odd one out

Breaking numbers up makes it easier to add them together.

On your toes Which gives the greater answer, 15 – 7 or 56 ÷ 8?

Written addition

There are three main ways of adding numbers together:

- ★ **in your head** – the best way if the numbers are manageable
- ★ **on paper** – the best way if the numbers are too big to handle in your head
- ★ **using a calculator** – the best way for tricky numbers if you need a quick answer and you are allowed to use one!

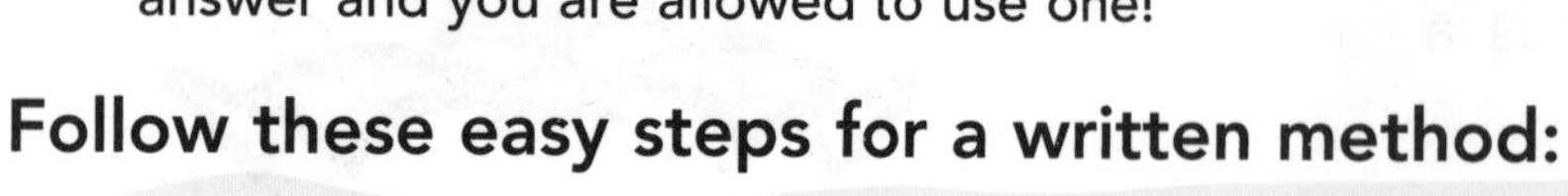

Follow these easy steps for a written method:

Ryan collects paperclips. He has 3896 silver ones and 749 coloured ones. How many has he got altogether?

Write the number in a column, lining up the units digits:

```
  3896
+  749
```

Start by adding from the units column. For any total over 9 just put the tens digit under the next column:

```
  3896
+  749
     5
    1
```

Don't forget to add these!

Now do the same with the tens column. Keep going to the left until all the columns have been added:

```
  3896
+  749
  4645
```

When you add decimals remember to line up the decimal points.

The method is the same as with whole numbers.

Bryan bought Ryan's collection for £234.56 and then spent £74.85 on the latest Japanese paper clips! How much did he spend altogether?

Write the numbers in a column, lining up the decimal points:

```
  234.56
+  74.85
```

Start by adding from the right-hand column:

```
  234.56
+  74.85
       1
      1
```

Keep going to the left until all the columns have been added:

```
  234.56
+  74.85
  309.41
```

Try these

1 What is the sum of 2743 and 1658?
2 95.86 + 217.9
3 3754
  + 6493
4 Total £681.50, £32.83 and £915.72.

Puzzle code

What is the missing digit?

```
  4□85
+ 2957
  7142
```

3 (T) 1 (S) 2 (R) 8 (P)

If you know your stuff...

174 + 681

362 + 493

426 + 419

382 + 473

...you'll spot the odd one out.

Write the letter in the grid on page 64.

This will help...

When you are adding decimals, write the decimal point in the answer space before you start. Make sure it is lined up with the ones above.

Estimate then calculate.

 On your toes What is the total of 65 and 66?

Mental subtraction

You often need to work out **differences** or subtract numbers in your head, particularly in shops or when you are measuring. Here are **three good methods**:

Breaking up the numbers into smaller chunks makes it easier:

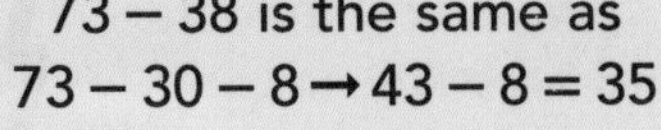

73 − 38 is the same as
73 − 30 − 8 → 43 − 8 = 35

Rounding numbers

is useful if the units digit is 8 or 9:

93 − 49 is the same as 93 − 50 then add 1 → 43 + 1 → 44

Counting on

is another good way of finding the difference between two numbers:

For 84 − 57, count on from 57 to 60 (hold the 3 in your head). 60 on to 84 is 24. Add 24 and 3, which is 27. This is a good method for finding the change from money amounts.

This will help...

Imagine a number line in your head and count on to find the difference: What is the difference between 56 and 93?

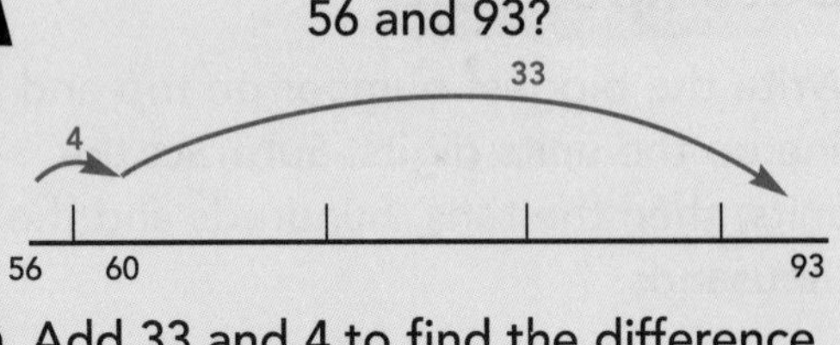

Add 33 and 4 to find the difference, which is 37.

You can use these methods when you subtract decimals too.

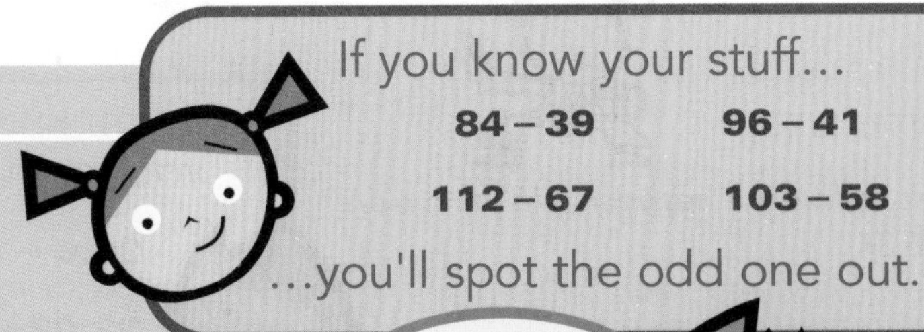

Try these

1 What is the difference between 47 and 91?
2 62 − ___ = 25
3 What is 8.8 − 3.6?
4 What is the change from £5 for a burger costing £1.48?

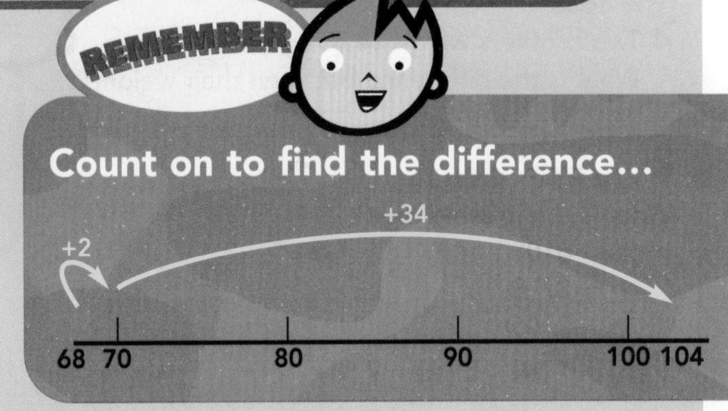

Puzzle code

What is the difference in weight between two puppies weighing 3.8 kg and 6.7 kg?

2.9 kg **(B)** 3.9 kg **(L)**
3.1 kg **(N)** 10.5 kg **(W)**

Write the letter in the grid on page 64.

On your toes What is the total of these three numbers: 1234, 5678, 9012?

Written subtraction

You can subtract large numbers using a calculator, but this isn't always possible so it's good to know how to do it on paper.

Choose between the two written methods, **decomposition** and **counting on** (below), to work out this example:

5483 people watch Big Eddy lose his first wrestling match.
756 people watch his next match...and he still loses.
How many fewer people are at the second match?

Decomposition

Write the biggest number on top and line up the units digits. Subtract the units, then the tens, hundreds and the thousands.

```
  5483        ⁴5̸ ₁4 ⁷8̸ ₁3
−  756      −    7  5  6
  4727         4  7  2  7
```

If a column has a smaller digit on top, then exchange a ten: in this case you're making 3 into 13 and 80 into 70.

Counting on

Find the difference between the numbers by counting on from the smaller to the larger.

Add up all the steps to find the difference:

```
  4483
   200
+   44
  4727
```

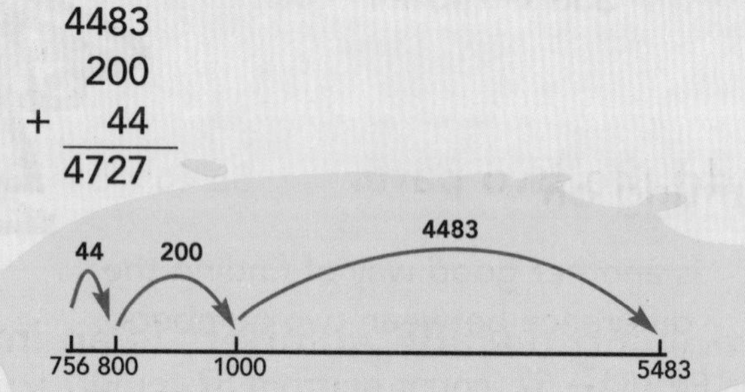

This will help...

When you subtract decimals you can use the same two methods. Remember to **line up the decimal points** if you use decomposition. Write the decimal point in the answer space before you start, lining it up with the ones above.

Try these

1 What is the difference between 3781 and 6209?
2 141.8 − 68.34
3 3402
− 1635
4 Two brothers weigh 34.45 kg and 27.83 kg. What is the difference between their weights?

Puzzle code

What is the missing digit?

```
  6103
− 37_8
  2305
```

1 **(C)** 0 **(N)** 5 **(A)** 9 **(O)**

Write the letter in the grid on page 64.

If you know your stuff...

38.6 − 18.93

32.07 − 13.4

39.83 − 21.16

34.42 − 15.75

...you'll spot the odd one out.

To subtract large numbers, such as

12345 − 6789

either DECOMPOSE or COUNT ON.

 On your toes What is the difference between 17.5 and 9.8?

Mental multiplication

If you know your table facts you should have no problem with multiplying big numbers in your head.

Sophie cycles 46 miles a day to work and back (she eats big breakfasts). How far does she cycle in five days?

The best thing to do is to think of 46 as 40 + 6 and multiply both numbers by 5.

It makes no difference which number you start with:

Start with the tens	$40 \times 5 = 200$
Multiply the units	$6 \times 5 = 30$
Add the two parts	So $46 \times 5 = 230$

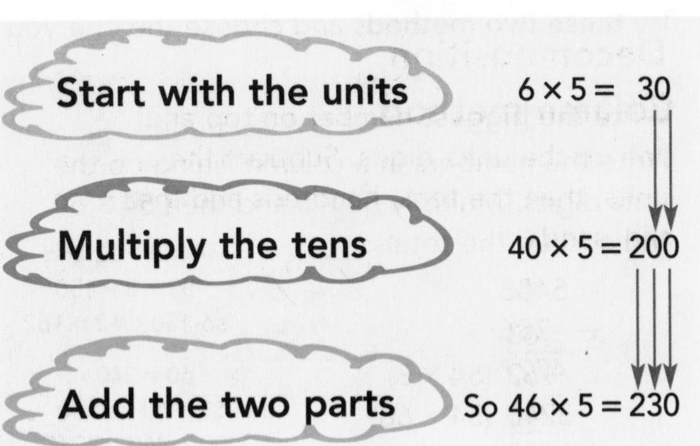

Multiplying decade numbers is an important part of being a speedy mental multiplier.

These are the tricky ones, so read them and learn them:

80×3	30×8	**240**	70×9	90×7	**630**	80×6	60×8	**480**
40×7	70×4	**280**	80×9	90×8	**720**	60×9	90×6	**540**
80×7	70×8	**560**	60×7	70×6	**420**	40×8	80×4	**320**

Try these

1 What is 39×7?
2 Which is larger, 44×6 or 66×4?
3 A chocolate bar weighs 86 g.
What do 4 bars weigh?
4 A tub of margarine costs 58p.
What do 6 tubs of margarine cost?

If you know your stuff…

48×9

54×8

66×7

72×6

…you'll spot the odd one out.

Multiplication – break it up into tens and ones.

Puzzle code

Which answer is nearest to 200?

35×8 **(S)** 27×7 **(P)** 51×4 **(O)** 64×3 **(R)**

Write the letter in the grid on page 64.

On your toes What is the difference between Mount Everest (8846 m) and the Matterhorn (4477 m)?

Written multiplication

Multiplying with large numbers is tricky to do in your head, but there are two methods that work well on paper.

The important thing is that both written methods for multiplying large numbers involve breaking numbers up and multiplying each part.

A budget airline charges £54 for a flight to Rome. If it has 63 passengers, how much are the passengers paying in total?

Try these two methods and choose the one you prefer.

Column method

Write the numbers in a column, lining up the units digits. Multiply 54×3 and then 54×60 and add up the totals:

$$\begin{array}{r} 54 \\ \times \quad 63 \\ \hline 162 \\ 3240 \\ \hline 3402 \end{array}$$

162 (54×3) — $4 \times 3 = 12$ and $50 \times 3 = 150$ so $150 + 12 = 162$

3240 (54×60) — $4 \times 60 = 240$ and $50 \times 60 = 3000$ so $3000 + 240 = 3240$

3402 — Add together 162 and 3240

The total is £3402.

Grid method

Write the numbers round a grid, breaking up each number into tens and units:

	50	4
60		
3		

Multiply each pair of numbers to complete the grid, then add up each row:

	50	4	
60	3000	240	→ 3240
3	150	12	→ 162

Add up the two totals:

	50	4	
60	3000	240	→ 3240
3	150	12	→ 162
			3402

The total is £3402.

This will help...

Before you start on a calculation, estimate an approximate answer. You'll then know if you're way out with your answer (a common mistake is to have too many or not enough zeros).

Example:

37×52 is approximately 40×50, which is 2000. So the answer should be just under 2000.

Larger calculations, such as 3485×8 and 295×64, can be worked out using the same methods. Choose the one you prefer and practise it.

Try these

1. What is 56×84?
2. A bag holds 45 nails. If a box holds 36 bags, how many nails are in the box?
3. A jar of marmite costs 87p. What will 28 jars cost?
4. What is 345×62?

If you know your stuff...

60×400

800×30

200×120

160×15

...you'll spot the odd one out.

Break up the numbers multiply out each part and then add them for the total.

Puzzle code

Ali saves £27 a week to buy a motorbike costing £972. How many weeks will he need to save?

30 (T) 42 (R) 39 (M) 36 (K)

Write the letter in the grid on page 64.

 On your toes Is 45×67 more or less than 3000?

Mental division

Division is one of those areas of maths that can be disguised in lots of different ways – so be careful!

48 brave people are launched into space to set up a colony on Venus. If equal numbers are put on to 6 spaceships, how many people are on each spaceship?

This could be written as $48 \div 6$ or $6\overline{)48}$ or $\frac{48}{6}$...

they all mean the same thing: **48 divided by 6**.
The strange thing is: multiplication will help you find the answer.

How many sixes in 48? $8 \times 6 = 48$ so there are 8 people on each spaceship.

Division is the inverse or opposite of multiplication.

These trios show the link:

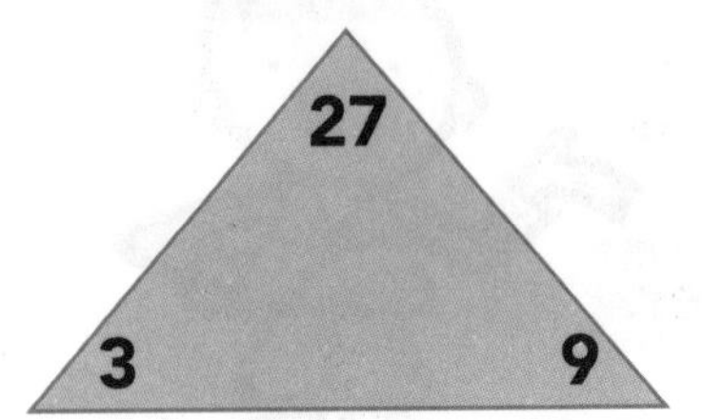

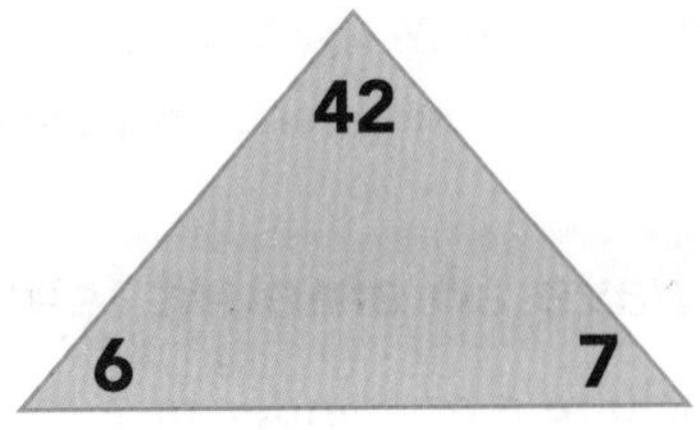

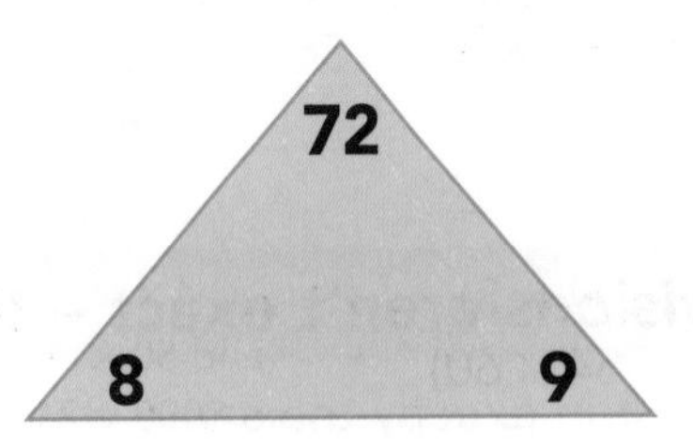

$3 \times 9 = 27$

$27 \div 9 = 3$

$27 \div 3 = 9$

$7 \times 6 = 42$

$42 \div 6 = 7$

$42 \div 7 = 6$

$8 \times 9 = 72$

$72 \div 9 = 8$

$72 \div 8 = 9$

Once you know this, then dividing larger numbers can still be done in your head by using multiplication. Use the facts you know to break the numbers up:

$105 \div 5$ (20×5 is 100, so the answer is 21)

$96 \div 3$ (30×3 is 90, so the answer is 32)

$168 \div 4$ (40×4 is 160, so the answer is 42)

This will help...

If you are given a missing number problem, use the numbers you are given to help work it out.

$54 \div \_\_\_ = 6.$

How many sixes in 54? The missing number is 9.

$4 \times \_\_\_ = 32$

How many fours in 32? The missing number is 8.

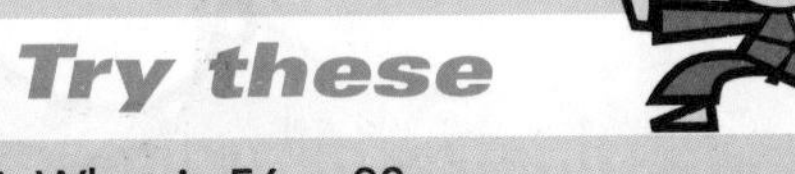

Try these

1 What is $56 \div 8$?
2 $6\overline{)78}$
3 $\_\_ \div 5 = 14$
4 $132 \div 4$

Puzzle code

Which of these numbers can be divided exactly by 9?

118 **(B)** 109 **(M)** 96 **(A)** 126 **(Y)** *Write the letter in the grid on page 64.*

If you know your stuff...

$56 \div 7$

$3\overline{)24}$

$\frac{81}{9}$

$64 \div 8$

...you'll spot the odd one out

Multiply to work out a division.

On your toes Is 37×6 more or less than 200?

Written division

Long division is a part of maths that can cause nightmares...

and that's just for the teachers! But it needn't be that bad. Just follow these steps:

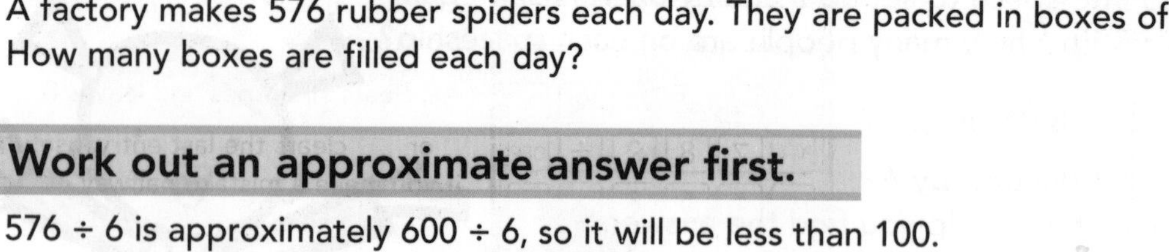

A factory makes 576 rubber spiders each day. They are packed in boxes of 6. How many boxes are filled each day?

Work out an approximate answer first.

576 ÷ 6 is approximately 600 ÷ 6, so it will be less than 100.

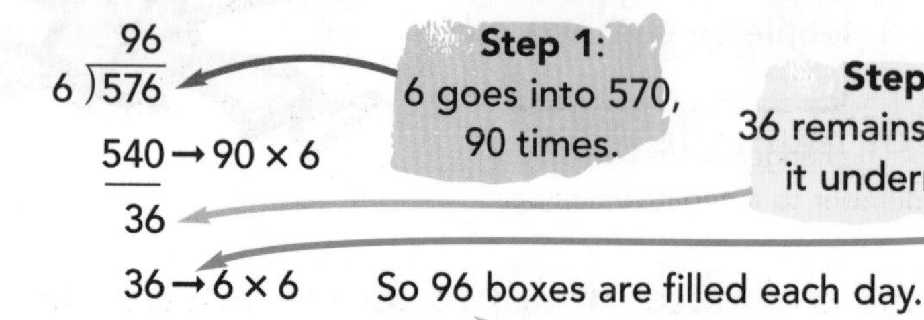

So 96 boxes are filled each day.

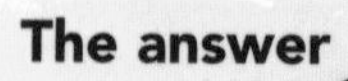

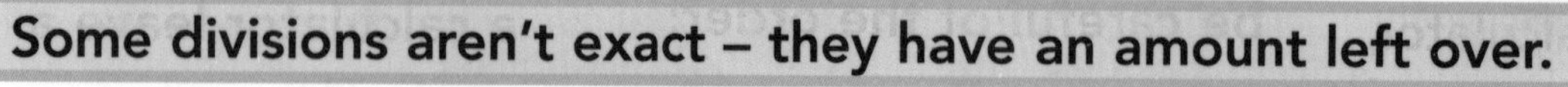

Some divisions aren't exact – they have an amount left over.

Work them out in exactly the same way, but include a remainder or a decimal. (These use the short method – see below.)

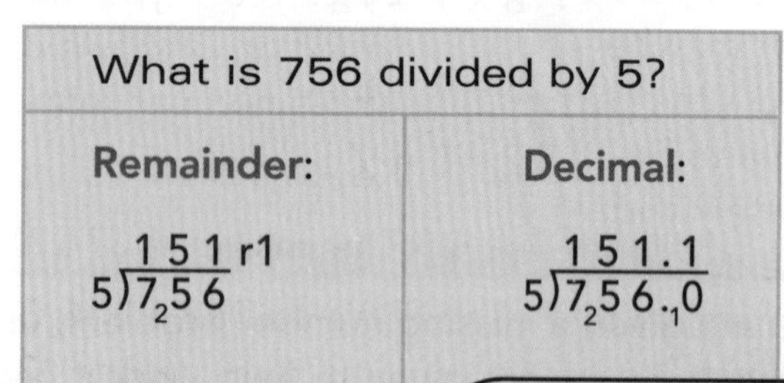

What is 756 divided by 5?	
Remainder:	**Decimal:**
$5\overline{)7_{2}56}$ = 151 r1	$5\overline{)7_{2}56._{1}0}$ = 151.1

This will help...

Go through the long method a few times, talking through each step. Once you understand it you can try writing a division using the shorter method:

$6\overline{)57_{3}6}$ = 96

There are 9 sixes in 570, with 30 left over. Write the 3 to make 36. There are 6 sixes in 36

Try these

1 Divide 372 by 4.
2 $9\overline{)5637}$
3 £879 is shared by 6 people. How much do they each get?
4 782.5 ÷ 5

If you know your stuff...

85 ÷ 6
49 ÷ 8
96 ÷ 5
74 ÷ 3

...you'll spot the odd one out.

Puzzle code

What is the remainder when 382 is divided by 7?

6 **(E)** 4 **(O)** 3 **(I)** 5 **(A)**

Write the letter in the grid on page 64.

Using a calculator

Some test questions allow you to use a calculator...great! But this doesn't mean you'll definitely get it right – you still have to do some thinking.

First of all, look at the question and make a decision. Is it easier to...

- work it out in your head
- use pen and paper
- use a calculator

If you want to use a calculator, make sure you know how to use these keys:

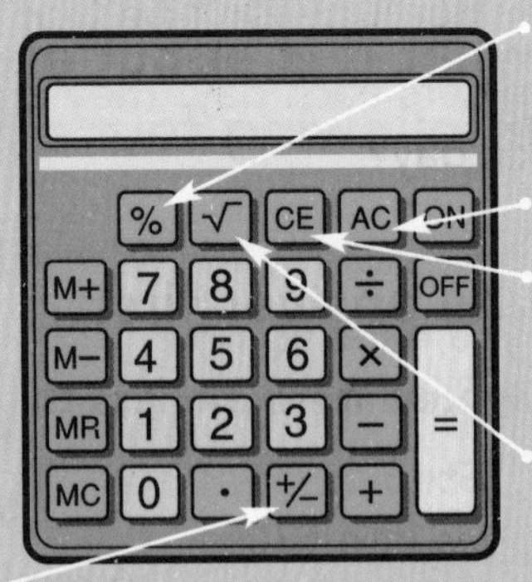

% **percentage**, e.g. to find 35% of £40, key in 40 × 35 × % is £14. Don't press =

AC clears all entries and leaves 0.

C or **CE** clears the last entry, useful if you make a mistake halfway through a sum

$\sqrt{\ }$ **square root** (opposite of square number), e.g. to find square root of 144, press 144 then the $\sqrt{\ }$ key

+/– changes a positive number to a negative number

Before you use the calculator, always estimate an approximate answer first.

When you solve money problems with a calculator, be careful of the zeros:

If you key in £7.62 + £4.78, the display reads 12.4. This means £12.40

A display of 0.93 means £0.93 or 93p.

A display of 6.38935 needs to be rounded to 2 decimal places: £6.39.

If you have brackets, be careful of the order:

If you key in (38 × 4) + (27 × 6) in the order the numbers are written, the answer may be 1074. This is wrong – the parts in the brackets have to be worked out separately and then added, so the actual answer is 314. Remember to work out the **brackets first**.

Division problems on a calculator leave a decimal remainder.

Be careful – you may want to round up or down or leave a whole number remainder.

Key in 6745 ÷ 18.

The answer is 374.7222222

This could be 374, 375, 374.72 or 374 remainder 13, depending on the question.

This will help...

Learn how to use the memory keys:

M+ adds numbers from display into memory.

M– subtracts numbers from display into memory.

MR recalls numbers from display back into display.

MC clears memory.

Use the memory keys for brackets: (3 × 6) + (4 × 5) = 38

Key in: 3 × 6 + 4 × 5 = If the answer is not 38 (is it 110?) then you need to use the memory key. Follow these instructions:

3 × 6 = M+ 4 × 5 = M+ MR 38

Try these

1. Calculate 34% of £255.
2. 1609.3 ÷ □ = 84.7
3. (32 × 5) + (92 ÷ 4)
4. Harry saves £1.35 each week. How much has he saved after 38 weeks?

Puzzle code

The area of a square is 196 cm². What is the length of each side?

14 cm **(U)** 24 cm **(B)** 16 cm **(N)** 49 cm **(S)**

Write the letter in the grid on page 64.

Estimate, calculate and check.

On your toes What is the remainder when 674 is divided by 8?

Problem solving

Revise wise

You may dread maths problems, but try not to panic – they are just sums in disguise.

When you read a word-problem try to 'picture' the problem – can you work out exactly what it is about and what is being asked? Always go through the following four stages:

1 Understand

Read the problem. What do you need to find out? You may want to jot down key ideas or words.

2 Plan

Sort out the calculations. Is it an addition, or a multiplication and a subtraction..? There may be more than one calculation. Write down the different calculations.

3 Estimate the answer

4 Solve

Work out the answer. Which mental or written methods will you use?

5 Look back

Check your work. Have you answered all the parts of the problem? Have you actually answered the question? (Read it again.)

With word problems you may need one, two or three calculations to get to the answer.

One-step problems

Sam buys three super-hero masks costing £6.75 each.

How much does he spend in total?

Two-step problems

Five bags of rabbit food have a total weight of 9500 g.

What is the weight of 3 bags of rabbit food?

Three-step problems

Entrance to the Spooky Cave costs £3.90 for adults and 85 p for children.

What is the total cost for a family of 2 adults and 3 children?

This is a 'unit' problem: find the cost or weight of a single item by dividing by 5 and then multiplying by 3.

This will help...

When you answer maths problems, **always show your working out** on the page. Even if you get the final answer wrong you may have parts of it correct. With a bit of luck you may even be given an extra mark!

Try these

1 6 bags of crisps cost £2.22. How much would 5 bags cost?
2 Kim buys 4 plants at 80p each. How much change would she get from £5?
3 How long is 792 hours in weeks and days?
4 I think of a number, take away 4 and then divide it by 8. The answer is 30. What was my number?

Puzzle code

Gemma has £9.45 more than Jack, who has £12.90. How much do they have altogether?

£22.35 **(R)** £32.80 **(M)** £35.25 **(W)** £31.80 **(S)** *Write the letter in the grid on page 64.*

 On your toes Use a calculator to work out 42% of £25.

Formulae and equations

Formulae, equations, algebra... some fun mathsy words! These all sound far more complicated than they really are... they only involve reading letters!

A formula (plural is formulae) uses letters to give a rule.

Made-up formula:

A formula for the number of worms (w) in apples (a) could be $w = 3a + 2$

So for 5 apples there would be 17 worms:

$w = (3 \times 5) + 2 = 17$

How many worms would there be in 8 apples?

Just put a number in instead of 'a' for a different number of apples.

Real formula:

perimeter $= p$
length of side $= l$
breadth of side $= b$

The formula for the perimeter of a rectangle is: $p = 2(l + b)$

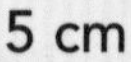

5 cm

4 cm

$p = 2(4 + 5) = 18$ cm

Equations use symbols or letters instead of numbers and show how things relate to each other.

You normally have to work out which number the letter stands for.

$\square + 4 = 9 \quad y + 4 = 9 \quad a + 4 = 9$

All these stand for 5.

$3y = 18$

This means 3 times y, as the × sign for multiplication isn't used in equations because it might look like a letter. So $y = 6$

This will help...

Equations need to stay balanced. If you add or take away a number from one side of the equals sign, do the same to the other side and the equation stays the same. It's a good way of working out the letter.

Try these

1. $3t - 5 = 10$
   $t =$ __
2. If $d = 4$
   Then $2d + 8 =$ __
3. $2a = b$
   If $a = 15$, what is b?
4. $6 + 3c = 30$
   $c =$ __

Puzzle code

$16 + m = n$

If $n = 30$, what is the value of m?

46 (R) 16 (E) 14 (I) 22 (A)

Write the letter in the grid on page 64.

If you know your stuff...

$4n - 6 = 10$

$c + 1 = 5$

$15 - 2a = 3$

$3z + 6 = 18$

...you'll spot the odd one out.

Letters stand for missing numbers.

On your toes If five iced buns cost £1.90, what is the cost of 3 buns?

Money

Money is a popular subject for maths questions so it's worth spending some time getting to grips with it.

When you add amounts in your head, it is sometimes easier to add the pounds and then the pence:

£3.60 + £5.90 → £8 add 150p → £9.50

When you subtract amounts or find differences in your head, it is sometimes easier to count on. This is good for working out change:

If you bought a piece of moon-rock for £6.85, what change would you get from £10?

£6.85 up to £7 is 15p. £7 up to £10 is £3.

£3 add 15p is £3.15.

£3.00
15p
£6.85 £7.00 £10

When you multiply and divide money amounts, estimate an approximate answer first.

If you can't work out the answer in your head, try these methods:

What is £9.18 × 5?

This is approximately £9 × 5 which is £45.

What is 4)£17.36 ?

This is approximately £17 divided by 4 which is £4.25.

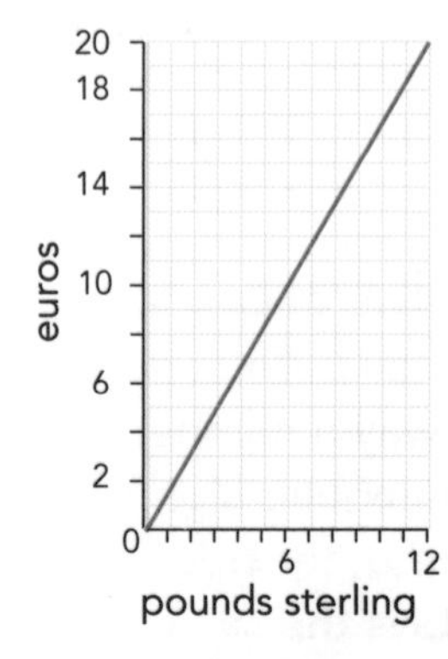

Exchange rates show the value of one currency against another.

The euro is now used by many European countries.

€1 is approximately equal to 60p.

This graph shows the conversion between the euro and pounds sterling.

What is the value of £3 in euros?

This will help...

If you need to work out totals or differences on paper, make sure the columns are in line.
The decimal points separating pounds from pence should be underneath each other.

  £78.64
– £19.37

Try these

1. A car costs £8132. If £645 is taken off the price as a discount, what will the car cost?
2. A bingo win of £948 is shared between 5 winners. How much do they each get?
3. What change would you get from £50 for 9 bottles of wine at £4.79 each?
4. What is the total cost of a tennis racket costing £37.39 and a tube of tennis balls at £6.84?

If you know your stuff… …you'll spot the odd one out

REMEMBER Estimate then calculate

Puzzle code

Which of these amounts cannot be made exactly with 4 coins?

£1.27 **(S)** 73p **(N)** £2.65 **(B)** £1.18 **(L)**

Write the letter in the grid on page 64.

 On your toes $3n + 5 = 26$ What is the value of n?

Probability

There is a good chance that you will get a probability question in a maths test... and that's what it's all about – chance.

We use probability words a lot:

What's the **likelihood** of mum's cooking not being burnt?

I think I'm **unlikely** to join the circus.

Juggling 18 saucepans is nearly **impossible**.

I'm **certain** you're going to win the 'beanbag on head' race.

It's **very likely** that our dog will lick your face if you smile at him.

We use a probability scale to show how likely an event is to happen:

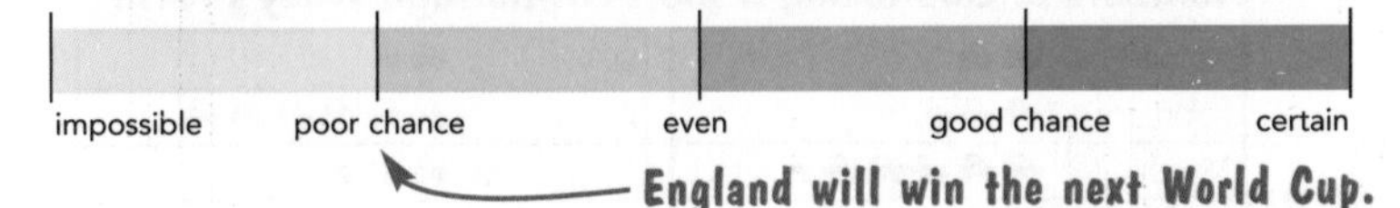

England will win the next World Cup.

Some probabilities are just an **opinion**, like this one. Others you can try to **prove** with experiments. This is much more mathematical!

This will help...

The probability scale can be shown with fractions, decimals or percentages.
An even chance is an equal chance of something happening or not happening. We also say a 1 in 2 chance, a 50% chance or a 50:50 chance.

Coin experiments

Coins can show heads or tails. This means there is a 1 in 2 or evens chance of showing heads. Look at this on the probability scale.

What if two coins were tossed? The possible combinations are:

HH
TT
HT
TH

So the chance of both showing heads are 1 in 4.

Dice experiments

Dice are useful for testing probabilities.

On a 1–6 dice, the probability of throwing a 6 is 1 in 6. It is the same chance for any number.

The chance of throwing an even number is 3 in 6, which is the same as 1 in 2 or evens.

What is the probability of throwing a 7?

What is the chance of throwing a 3 or 4?

Bead experiments

Look at this bag of beads.

There is a 3 in 8 chance of picking out a green bead. This is a less than evens chance.

There is a 1 in 2 or evens chance of picking a red bead.

What is the probability of picking out a yellow bead?

Where would this be on the probability scale?

With all these experiments you can try them out to see how accurate the probabilities are.

Roll a dice 60 times. You should roll 10 sixes. Does this happen?

Try these

What is the chance of landing on:

1 orange?
2 yellow?
3 either yellow or green?
4 green?

A good chance is greater than 1 in 2.

Puzzle code

In a pack of playing cards, what is the chance of picking a diamond?

1 in 13 **(T)** 1 in 8 **(N)** 1 in 4 **(L)** 1 in 16 **(S)**

Write the letter in the grid on page 64.

On your toes Slippers cost £17.49 a pair. If I need three pairs each year, how much do I spend annually?

Graphs and charts

Bar charts, pictograms, block graphs, pie charts... these are all ways of displaying information in an informative, simple way.

The important thing is to read all the parts of the graph before answering any questions.

Bar charts and block graphs have bars or columns.

1 Read the title: what is it about?

2 Look at the axis labels: what does each one show?

3 Work out the scale: do the numbers go up in 1s, 2s, 5s, 10s...?

4 Compare the bars: reading across, what is the value of each one?

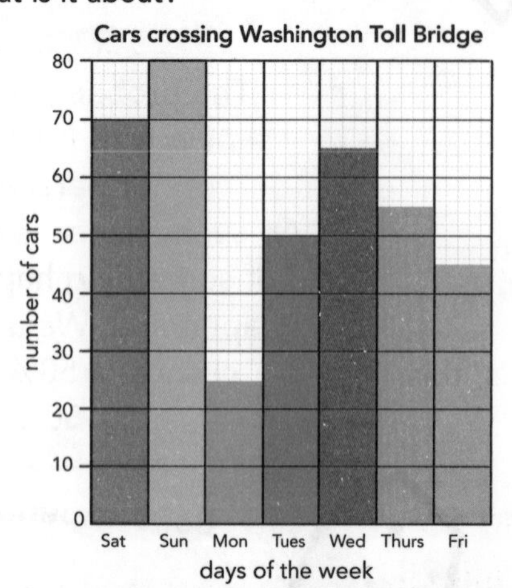

Pictograms are graphs that have pictures.

This pictogram shows the number of cars each month taking a short-cut through Wiley's Farm to avoid paying the toll fee of 5p.

Numbers of cars taking a short-cut through Wiley's Farm

January		July	
February		August	
March		September	
April		October	
May		November	
June		December	

= 10 cars

1 Read the title: what is it about?

2 Look at the scale: how many does each picture stand for?

3 Compare the number of cars for each month.

Pie charts are circles divided into sections.

Each section shows a number of items. This pie chart shows the types of vehicle taking a short-cut through Wiley's Farm in August. There were 600 vehicles altogether. How many buses took a shortcut?

Types of vehicles taking a short cut through Wiley's Farm

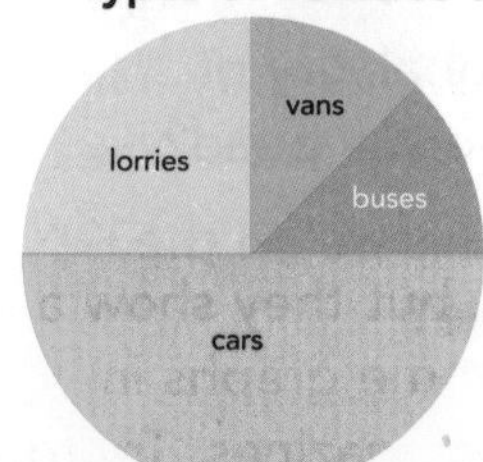

1 Read the title and any information: what is it about?

2 Find out the total: how many vehicles does the whole circle represent?

3 Compare the sections: what value is each of them?

4 Read the questions carefully: is the answer a fraction, a percentage or a number?

This will help...

Bar charts are sometimes called frequency charts. This means 'how many', so a frequency chart is a record of the number of items. These items can be grouped, which make them easier to compare.

A record was kept of the scores made when throwing two darts at a dart-board. A score between 26 and 30 was made 11 times.

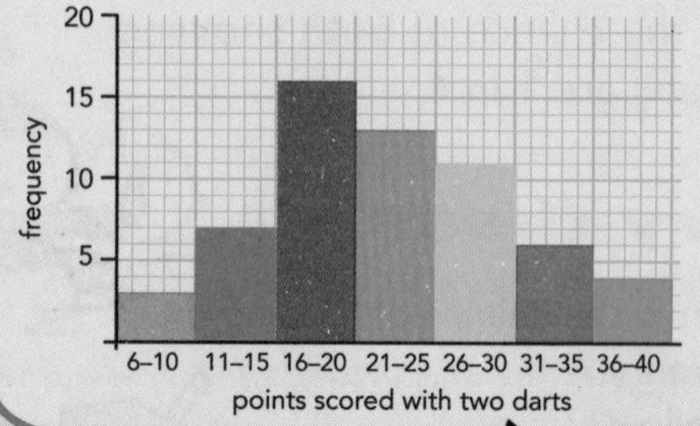

Try these

Use the graphs and charts on this page to answer these questions.

1 How many cars crossed the toll bridge on Wednesday?

2 What fraction of vehicles taking a short-cut in August were lorries?

3 Approximately how many vehicles took a short-cut in March?

4 How many cars took a short-cut in August?

Puzzle code

Look at the darts frequency chart in 'This will help...'. How many times did the points total between 16 and 20?

16 **(B)** 6 **(N)** 14 **(R)** 12 **(M)** *Write the letter in the grid on page 64.*

To understand graphs read all the information.

On your toes What is the chance of rolling an even number on a 1–6 dice?

Line graphs

Revise wise

Line graphs use lines instead of bars – obvious really!

They often have numbers for both axes and are simple to read.

1 Read the title and the labels on the axes so you know what it is about.
2 Go up from the horizontal axis to meet the line.
3 From this point read across to the vertical axis to give the value.
4 You can also go across and then down.

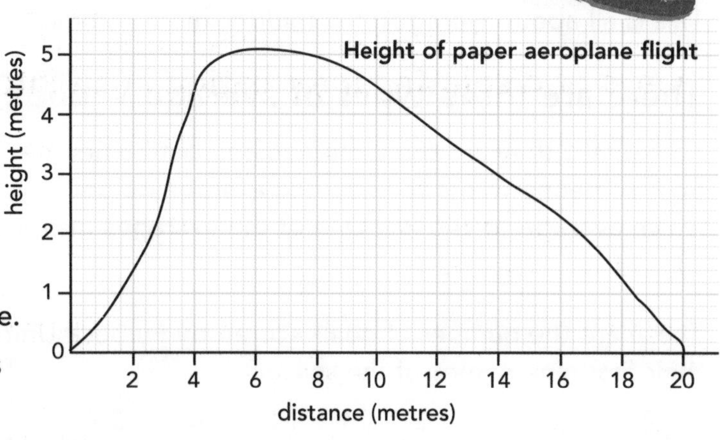

Conversion graphs are straight-line graphs that convert one amount to another.

For example, if you wanted to change litres into gallons, this graph would make it easy.

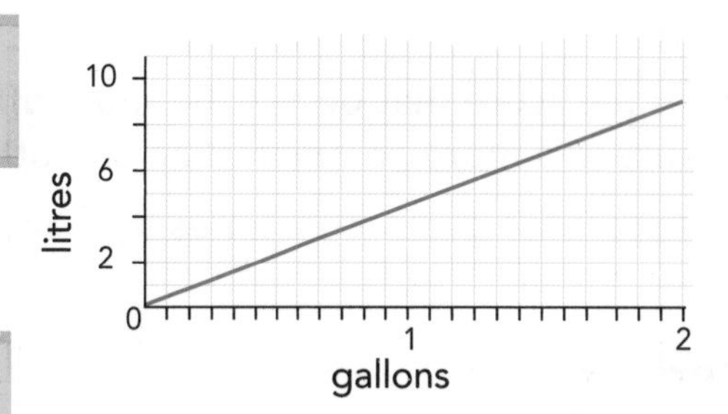

Time/distance graphs show the time taken to go a certain distance – also not too surprising!

This graph shows a train journey from London to Leeds.

Horizontal lines show where the train has stopped. How many stations do you think the train stopped at?

The steeper the line, the faster the journey – the train is travelling a greater distance over less time.

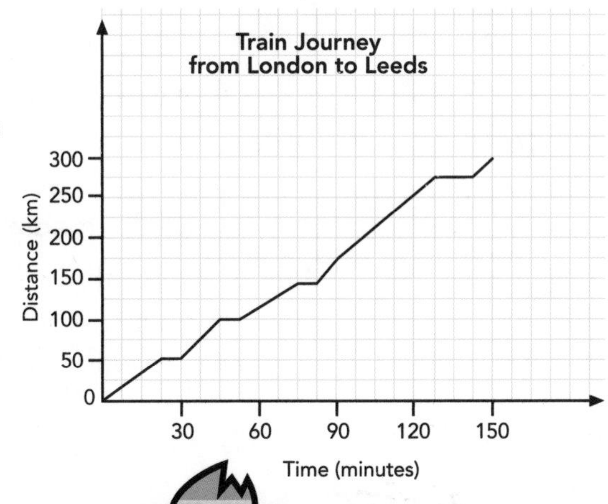

Speed is shown in kilometres per hour (km/h) or miles per hour (mph) – so this is a speed graph. The train travelled 300 km in 2.5 hours which is an average speed of 120 km/h.

This will help...

Many line graphs show a set of points or crosses joined by a line. This often means that the lines between the crosses don't show any real values, but they show a trend. Find some graphs in newspapers or magazines. Try to understand them and see what sort of graphs they are.

Try these

Use the graphs and charts on this page to answer these questions:

1 What height was the paper aeroplane after it had travelled 8 metres?
2 How many gallons is approximately equal to 20 litres?
3 After how many minutes had the London–Leeds train travelled 100 km?
4 How far had the London–Leeds train travelled after 1hr 30 mins?

REMEMBER

Read up from the horizontal axis, then across to the vertical

Puzzle code

Write the letter in the grid on page 64.

How far did the paper aeroplane (in the first example) travel before landing?

6 metres **(A)** 20 metres **(E)** 18 metres **(G)** 2 metres **(R)**

On your toes What is a frequency chart?

Mode, median and mean

This is all about averages: the middle, most common, normal number from a set.

There are three types of average – mode, median and mean.

Sometimes they are the same number, but sometimes they are different. So if someone wants to know the average height in your class, it is worth deciding which average to choose. One of the averages may make you above average in height!

These are the number of goals scored by Fulbeck United FC in their first nine games of the season:

2 6 4 2 1 2 4 5 1

This will help...

Always rearrange the numbers and list them in order of size to help work out any type of average. This will show the range which tells us how much the information is spread. To find the range, find the difference between the smallest and the largest amount. So the range for these goals scored is 6 take away 1 which is 5.

Mode

This is the score that occurs the most often. It is an average because it is more common than any other one.

They scored 2 goals more times than any other so the mode is 2.

Median

The median is the middle number.

To work out the median:

- Put the numbers in order from smallest to largest: 1, 1, 2, 2, 2, 4, 4, 5, 6
- Find the middle number: 1, 1, 2, 2, **2**, 4, 4, 5, 6

So 2 is the median number.

If there is an even number of items and you need to work out the median, you take the 2 middle numbers, add them together and divide by 2.

Mean

This is what most people think of as an average: the mean average.

mean = total ÷ the number in the set

Add up the total number of goals:

$1 + 1 + 2 + 2 + 2 + 4 + 4 + 5 + 6 = 27$

There were 9 matches.

$27 \div 9 = 3$

The mean average is 3.

So the mode and median both had 2 as the average number of goals scored. But the mean wasn't mean at all – the mean was 3 goals per game... not bad at all!

Try these

Look at this set of shoe sizes for a group of 7 friends: 8 9 8 4 7 8 5

1. What is the range of these shoe sizes?
2. What is the mode?
3. What is the median?
4. What is the mean?

If you know your stuff...
mode
mean
median
range
...you'll spot the odd one out

Mode = most often

Median = middle

Mean = total and divide

Puzzle code

What is the mean of these five heights?

100 cm 90 cm 110 cm 130 cm 170 cm

110 cm **(I)** 130 cm **(M)** 120 cm **(A)** 150 cm **(X)**

Write the letter in the grid on page 64.

 On your toes What does mph stand for?

Length

Revise wise

We measure length using lots of different units: millimetres, centimetres, metres, kilometres, inches, feet, yards, miles...

It is important to have an idea in your head of the rough size of each of these. There is no point in measuring the length of your garden in millimetres, and measuring the height of a plant in kilometres would be daft – unless it was a magic beanstalk.

Try to remember these equivalent measures:

1 centimetre (cm) = 10 millimetres (mm)

1 metre (m) = 100 cm = 1000 mm

1 kilometre (km) = 1000 m

Once you know these, converting from one unit to another is quite easy.

An octopus' tentacles measure about 2.8 m. This is 280 cm or 2800 mm

A whale's intestines are about 0.4 km long. This is 400 m or 40000 cm.

Do you notice that this always means multiplying or dividing by 10, 100 or 1000? Always check that the conversion makes sense:

$$2.8\,\text{m} \times 100 = 280\,\text{cm}$$
$$280\,\text{cm} \times 10 = 2800\,\text{mm}$$

This will help...

You may notice that older people still sometimes use imperial measures. They are not as sensible as metric measures which are easy to convert from one unit to another, but for some strange reason they are still used. Try to learn these and think of times when you may have used them:

12 inches = 1 foot
1.6 km is about 1 mile
2.5 cm is about 1 inch
3 feet = 1 yard
30 cm is about 1 foot
3 feet is just under 1 metre

Remember it helps to know that...

milli means one thousandth ($\frac{1}{1000}$)

centi means one hundredth ($\frac{1}{100}$)

kilo means one thousand.

Try these

1. What is 250 m in km?
2. Which is the longer distance: 85 mm or 0.85 cm?
3. A car is travelling at 50 miles per hour. Approximately what is this in km per hour?
4. Approximately how long is 6 inches in centimetres?

If you know your stuff...
425 mm
42.5 cm
4.25 m
0.425 m
...you'll spot the odd one out.

millimetre
↓
centimetre
↓
metre
↓
kilometre

Puzzle code

Which of these measurements is incorrect for the length of this line?

Write the letter in the grid on page 64.

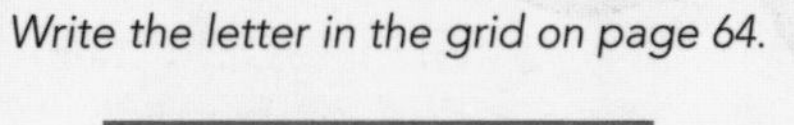

6.8 cm **(N)** 6 cm 8 mm **(T)**
68 mm **(R)** 0.68 m **(M)**

On your toes What is the mean of this set of lengths: 11 m, 8 m, 5 m, 9 m, 17 m?

Mass

Mass and weight are used as if they are identical and, for you and me, they may as well be. But, there is a difference.

Mass is a measure of the amount of 'matter' that an object contains. We mostly use kilograms and grams to measure mass.

Weight is a measure of the force that is produced on an object by gravity. This is mostly measured in newtons.

Mass and weight are connected. On Earth your mass and weight are the same. But weight is affected by the pull of gravity, so your mass on the moon would be the same as on Earth but your weight would be different.

Did you know that you are supposed to use commas instead of decimal points for measures? So it should be 8,35 kg. Don't worry though, you are allowed to use a decimal point, as long as it is on the line and not half-way up (for example 8.35 kg).

Make sure you know these:

1 kilogram (kg) 5 1000 grams (g)

1 tonne 5 1000 kg

Remember, to convert between them, multiply or divide by 10, 100 or 1000.

This will help...

We still have some imperial units for mass.
Try to learn these:

1 ounce = 30 grams

2.2 pounds = 1 kilogram

There are 16 ounces in a pound.

This $3\frac{1}{2}$ tonne truck weighs 3.5 tonnes (strangely enough!) or 3500 kg.

The sacks each weigh 8.2 kg or 8200 g.

Try these

1. 2.04 kg = __ g
2. Which is lighter, 850 g or 0.8 kg?
3. A recipe asks for 8 oz of butter. How much is this in grams?
4. Jimmy, a heavyweight wrestler, weighs in at 220 pounds. What is this in kilograms?

If you know your stuff…

6500 g

6kg 50 g

$6\frac{1}{2}$kg

6.5 kg

…you'll spot the odd one out

Puzzle code

How heavy is this cake?

3080 g **(E)** 3 kg 80 g **(O)**
3.8 kg **(A)** 3.08 kg **(U)**

Write the letter in the grid on page 64.

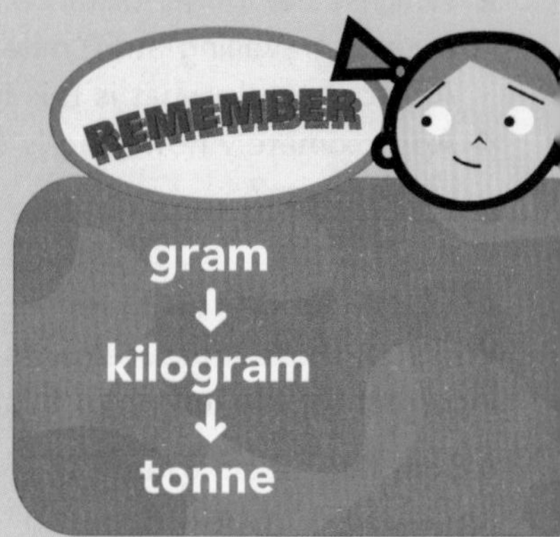

 On your toes The world long jump record is almost 30 feet. Approximately what is this in metres?

Capacity

Litres, millilitres and centilitres are the standard metric units of capacity.

It is a good idea to get a mental picture of the size of a litre. Fill a 1 litre jug with water. From that you can then visualise centilitres, which are $\frac{1}{100}$ of 1 litre (fairly small) and millilitres, which are $\frac{1}{1000}$ of 1 litre (very small).

Think of the relationship between metres, centimetres and millimetres and it gives you an idea when comparing litres, centilitres and millilitres.

1 litre (l) = 1000 millilitres (ml)

1 millilitre = $\frac{1}{1000}$ litre (l)

1 centilitre (cl) = $\frac{1}{100}$ litre = 10 ml

Remember, to convert between them, multiply or divide by 10, 100 or 1000.

My bread-making machine needs 350 ml or 3.5 cl of water.

This fabulous jar holds 2.2 l of olive oil, which is 2200 ml.

This will help...

We still have some imperial measures for capacity. You may have used pints or gallons before. Try to learn these equivalent amounts

8 pints = 1 gallon

1.75 pints = 1 litre

4.5 litres = 1 gallon

Try these

1 What is 6800 ml in litres?
2 A lemonade bottle holds 250 cl. If 150 ml is drunk, how much is left?
3 A 4 litre milk container holds approximately how many pints?
4 3.65 l = __ ml

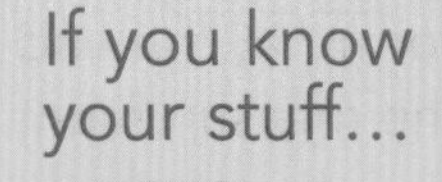

If you know your stuff…

7250 ml

7.25 l

725 cl

7 litres 25 ml

…you'll spot the odd one out.

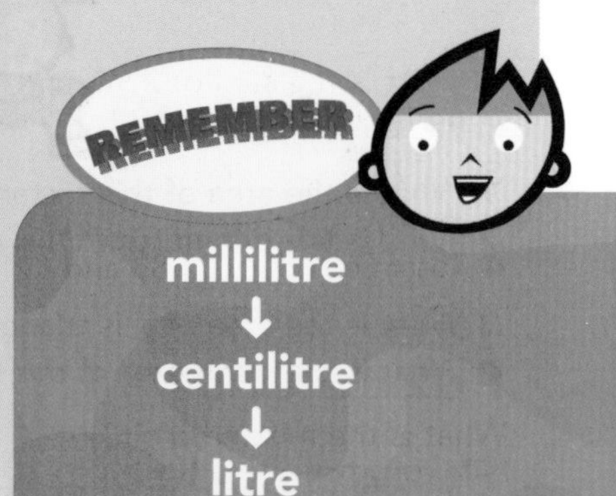

Puzzle code

How much liquid is in this jug?

0.65 l **(T)**

750 ml **(D)**

60 cl **(R)**

605 ml **(X)**

Write the letter in the grid on page 64.

On your toes A kitten weighs 350 g, then grows to 1.7 kg. How much weight has it increased by?

Perimeter and area

Perimeter and area are often linked, so don't get them confused.

The perimeter is the distance all the way round a shape. The area of a shape is the amount of surface that it covers.

A centimetre square grid can be used to show this.

Perimeter: 14 cm
Area: 8 cm^2

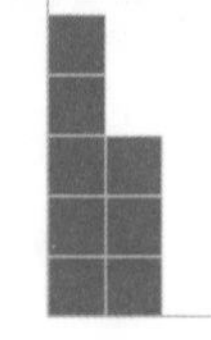

If the shape has curved sides, work out the area by counting all the squares that are bigger than a half. You can use a piece of string to work out the perimeter.

To find the area of compound shapes, split them into rectangles.

Find the area of each part and then add them together.

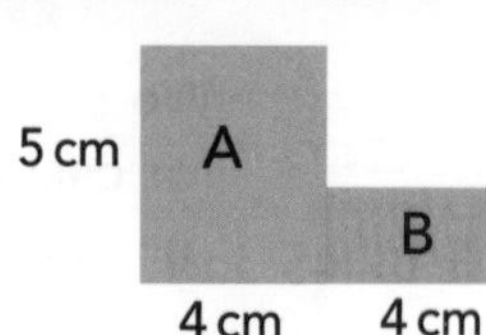

Area of rectangle A is 4×5 cm = 20 cm^2

Area of rectangle B is 4×2 cm = 8 cm^2

Total area = 28 cm^2

Remember: the perimeter is the distance around the whole outside edge, not round each rectangle.

Don't forget the cm^2 or m^2 at the end of the measurement for area.

Rectangles are great shapes for finding the perimeter and area. Look at this rectangle.

Find the **perimeter** using this simple formula:

$2(l + b) = 2(6 + 9) = 2 \times 15 = 30$ m

Written in words this says add together the length (l) and breadth (b) and then multiply by 2.

The **area** is found by multiplying the length by breadth. So $l \times b = 9 \times 6 = 54\ m^2$

This will help...

You might be asked to find the area of a right-angled triangle. If you picture this as half a rectangle then it makes it easy:

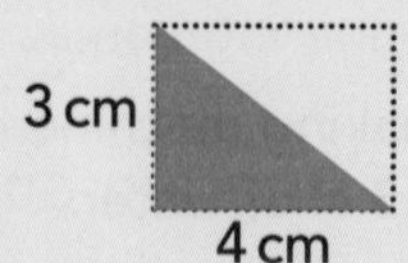

$\frac{1}{2}(l \times b) = \frac{1}{2}$ of $12 = 6\ cm^2$

So for this shape, just find the area of each part and then add them together.

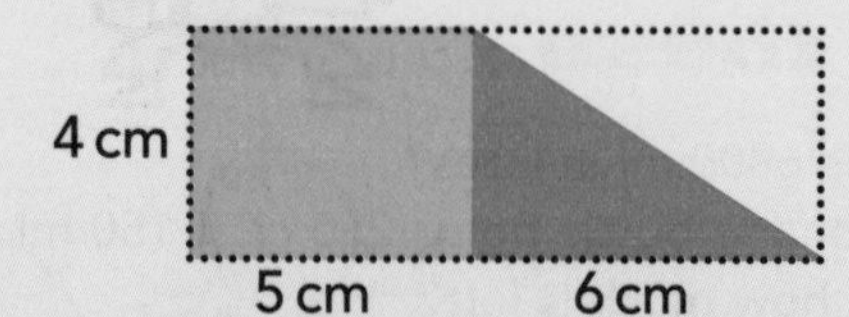

Area of rectangle is 5×4 cm = 20 cm^2
Area of triangle is $\frac{1}{2} \times 6 \times 4$ cm = 12 cm^2

Total area = 32 cm^2

area = length × breadth
perimeter = 2 × (length + breadth)

Try these

7 cm
9 cm

1 What is the area of this rectangle?
2 What is the perimeter of this rectangle?

10 cm
8 cm
6 cm

3 What is the area of this triangle?
4 What is the perimeter of this triangle?

Puzzle code

What is the area of this shape?

44 cm^2 **(C)** 48 cm^2 **(H)**
22 cm^2 **(S)** 54 cm^2 **(E)**

3 cm
10 cm
6 cm
3 cm

Write the letter in the grid on page 64.

 On your toes If a glass holds 330 ml of water, approximately how many glassfuls is 1 litre?

Reading the time

We read the time using an analogue clock with hands or a digital clock with numbers.

Both these clocks show 4.25 or 25 minutes past 4.

Analogue time

Digital time

If you struggle with reading an analogue clock, forget reading 'to' the hour and read it like digital time. Look at the hour hand to see which hour has just been passed,and then say the minutes past that hour. So this says 3.40 or 40 minutes past 3.

On timetables and in TV guides you may notice 'am' and 'pm' written after the time. am stands for ante meridiem and means morning – from 12 midnight to 12 noon. pm stands for post meridiem and means afternoon – from 12 noon to 12 midnight.

Here's a good way to remember which is which: in the alphabet, the 'a' in 'am' comes before 'p' in 'pm', and morning comes before afternoon.

This will help...

You may get a question like this in a test:
Bonzo buries his bone at 2.35 pm. He has a quick nap and then digs it up again at 4.20 pm. How long is the bone buried for?
Try sketching a quick timeline:

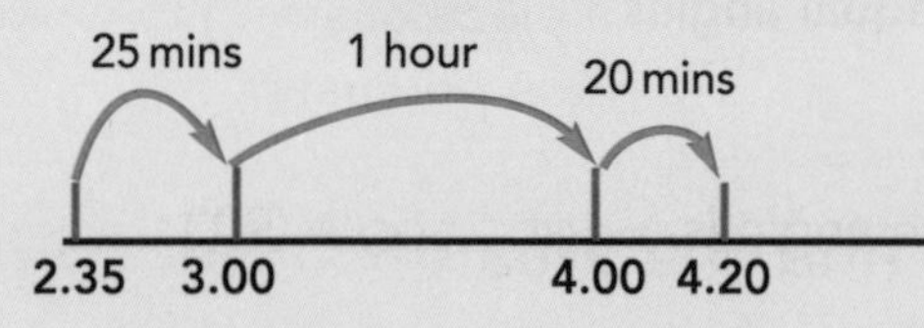

So the total time is 1 hour 45 minutes.

Instead of using am and pm, digital clocks and timetables can show 24-hour time.

24-hour time goes from 00:00 to 24:00. So 7.45am is 07:45 and 7.45pm is 19:45.

To read 24-hour time, am times look the same, but you add 12 hours to pm times.

You always use four numbers when you write the 24-hour clock.

1 am	2 am	3 am	4 am	5 am	6 am	7 am	8 am	9 am	10 am	11 am	12 am	1 pm	2 pm	3 pm	4 pm	5 pm	6 pm	7 pm	8 pm	9 pm	10 pm	11 pm	12 midnight
01:00	02:00	03:00	04:00	05:00	06:00	07:00	08:00	09:00	10:00	11:00	12:00	13:00	14:00	15:00	16:00	17:00	18:00	19:00	20:00	21:00	22:00	23:00	00:00

Try these

1 What time does this show?
2 This is the time that Archie goes to bed. What is it in 24-hour time?
3 Look at this train timetable.

London	York	Newcastle	Edinburgh
15:35	17:41	18:43	20:16

How long is the journey from York to Newcastle?
4 How long is the journey from London to Edinburgh?

If you know your stuff...

...you'll spot the odd one out.

REMEMBER

Read the time as minutes past the hour.

Puzzle code

The video is set for 55 minutes. If it starts recording at 13:42, when will it stop?

14:47 (Y) 13:97 (A) 14:27 (E) 14:37 (S) *Write the letter in the grid on page 64.*

On your toes A square has an area of 49 cm². What is the perimeter of the square?

2D Shapes

Any flat shape with straight sides is called a polygon.

Regular polygons are shapes with all sides and angles equal.

Regular triangle: 3 equal sides   Regular quadrilateral: 4 equal sides

Regular pentagon: 5 equal sides   Regular hexagon: 6 equal sides

Learn the features of these triangles...

equilateral
3 equal sides
3 equal angles

isosceles
2 equal sides
2 equal angles

right-angled
one angle is a right angle (90°)

scalene
no equal sides
no equal angles

Do you know these quadrilaterals?

square
4 equal sides
4 equal angles

rectangle
2 pairs of equal sides
4 right angles

rhombus
4 equal sides
opposite angles equal
opposite sides parallel

parallelogram
opposite sides are equal and parallel

kite
two pairs of adjacent sides are equal

trapezium
one pair of parallel sides

This will help...

To work out the name of a shape, look at the sides and then at the angles.
Sides → How many? Equal length? Parallel?
Angles → Any equal? Any right angles?

Try these

1 What is the name of this quadrilateral?
2 What is the name of this triangle?
3 How many sides has a hexagon?
4 What is special about a regular polygon?

REMEMBER

The name of the polygon tells you the number of sides.

tri- 3   hept- 7
quad- 4   oct- 8
pent- 5   non- 9
hex- 6   dec- 10

Puzzle code

Which shape has a pair of parallel sides?

 (L) 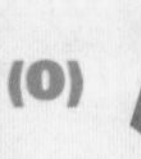 (O)  (R)  (G)

 On your toes A film starts at 7.40pm and finishes at 9.12pm. How long does the film last?

3D Shapes

Revise wise

3-dimensional shapes are solid shapes.

The two important things are to know the names and properties of shapes.

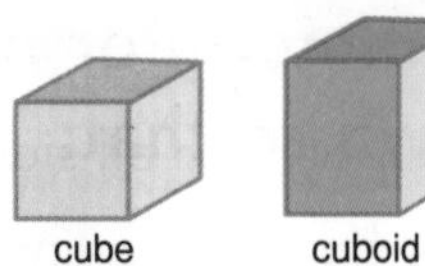
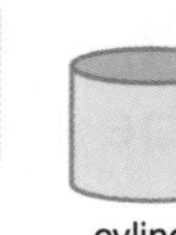

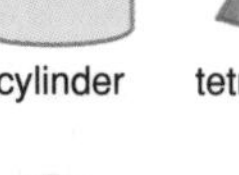

cube cuboid cylinder tetrahedron

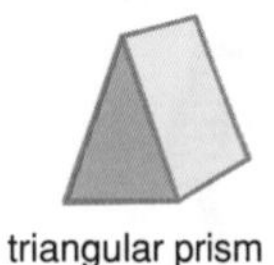
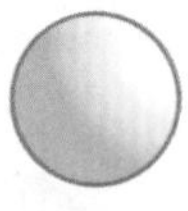
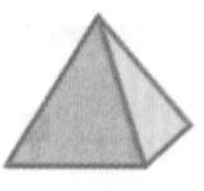

cone triangular prism sphere square-based pyramid

Polyhedra are 3D shapes made from lots of polygons (2D shapes with straight sides).

Each polyhedron has faces, edges and vertices:

- a face is flat and is a polygon
- an edge is a straight line where two faces meet
- a vertex (two or more vertices) is the point or corner where three or more edges meet.

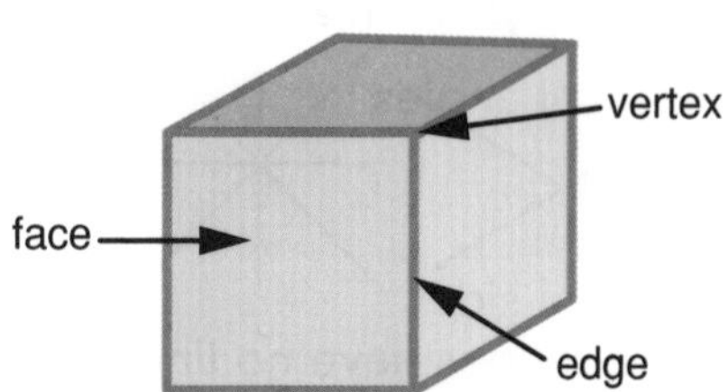

To describe properties of shapes, look at the shapes and number of faces, number of edges and number of vertices.

A cube has 6 square faces, 12 edges and 8 vertices.

Describe a triangular prism in this way.

The net of a shape is what it looks like when it is opened out flat. Try to picture opening out a box. If you closed it up you could open it again so that the net looks different. This is important – shapes can have more than one net.

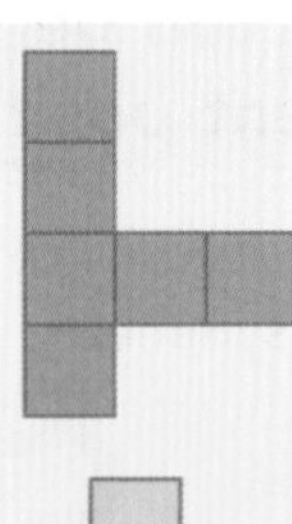

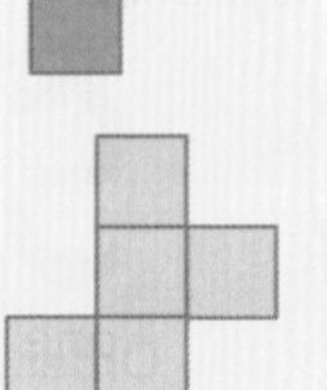

This will help...

Prisms can be tricky to recognise. They always have two parallel, identical 'end' faces and rectangle 'side' faces. The end-shapes can be any polygon and a prism can be cut into slices which are all the same shape.

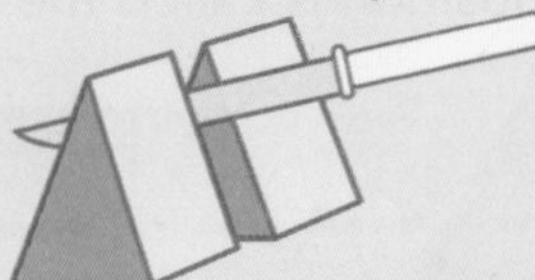

This is a triangular prism, but cubes and cuboids are also special prisms.

Try these

1. Which shape has four triangular faces?
2. What is the name of this shape?
3. How many vertices does a cuboid have?
4. Which shape-net is this?

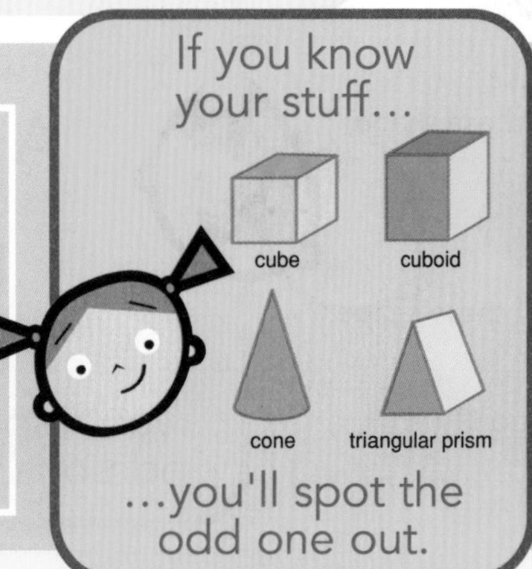

Make sure you know what these are:

- **faces**
- **edges**
- **vertices**

Puzzle code

Which of the following shapes has 5 faces, 5 vertices and 8 edges?

square-based pyramid **(E)** tetrahedron **(B)** triangular prism **(S)** cuboid **(C)**

Write the letter in the grid on page 64.

On your toes Which quadrilateral has 4 equal sides and no right angles?

Symmetry

A shape has line symmetry or reflective symmetry if a line can be drawn so that:

- when the shape is folded along the line, one half fits exactly over the other half

- when a mirror is placed on the line, the half shape and its reflection show the whole shape.

Some shapes have more than one line of symmetry:

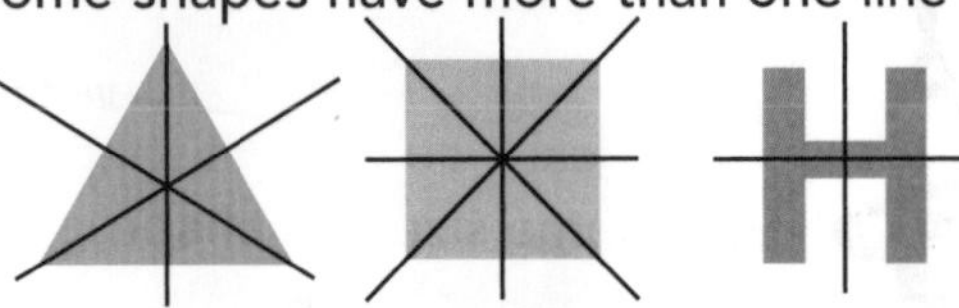

Some shapes have no lines of symmetry:

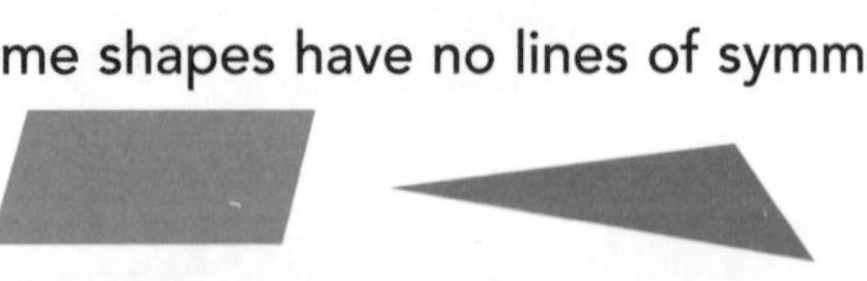

This will help...

Tracing paper is useful for checking if a shape has line or rotational symmetry.
Just trace the shape and...

- for line symmetry, fold it to see if both sides fold exactly together
- for rotational symmetry just lay the tracing paper over the original, rotate the shape and count the times it fits exactly into the original shape.

A shape has rotational symmetry if it can be rotated and looks the same in different positions.

The number of times a shape is rotated before it returns to its original position is called the order of rotational symmetry.

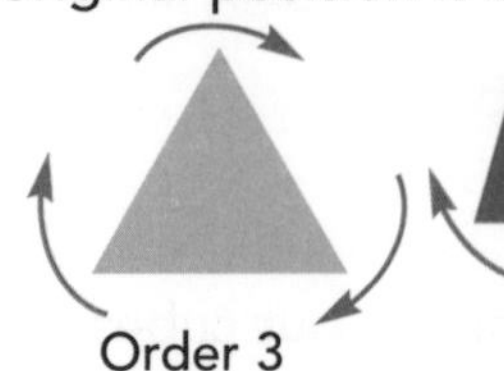

Order 3 Order 2 Order 4 Order 2

If a shape has no rotational symmetry then it has order 1:

Try these

How many lines of symmetry have each of these shapes?

1  2 

What is the order of rotational symmetry of these shapes?

3  4 X

If you know your stuff...

A D E F

...you'll spot the odd one out.

Puzzle code

Which of these shapes has rotational symmetry and no line symmetry?

  (D)   (E)  (N)  (T)

Write the letter in the grid on page 64.

 On your toes How many faces are there on a hexagonal prism?

Moving shapes

Shapes can be moved around in three different ways: rotation, reflection, translation

Rotation: a shape can be rotated about a point, clockwise or anti-clockwise.

This is rotated around point X.

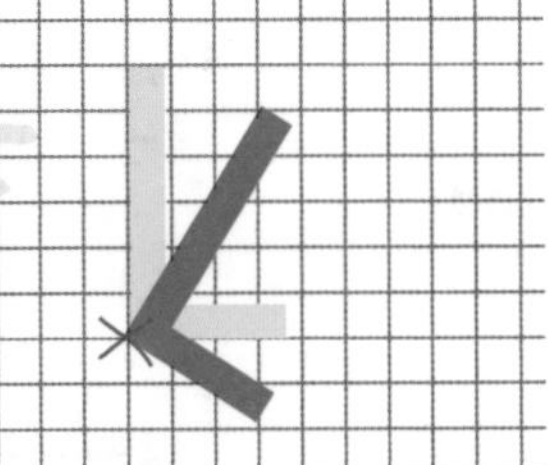

Reflection: this is when a shape is flipped over so it is a reflection in a mirror line.

This is reflected in the mirror line.

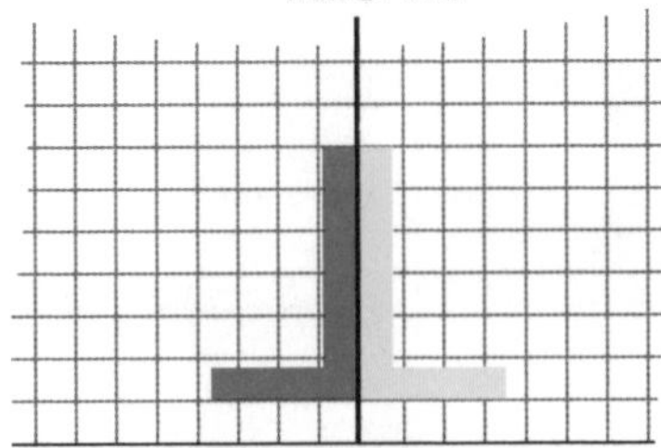

Translation: this is when a shape slides without rotating or flipping over.

This has been translated 4 squares across and 3 squares down.

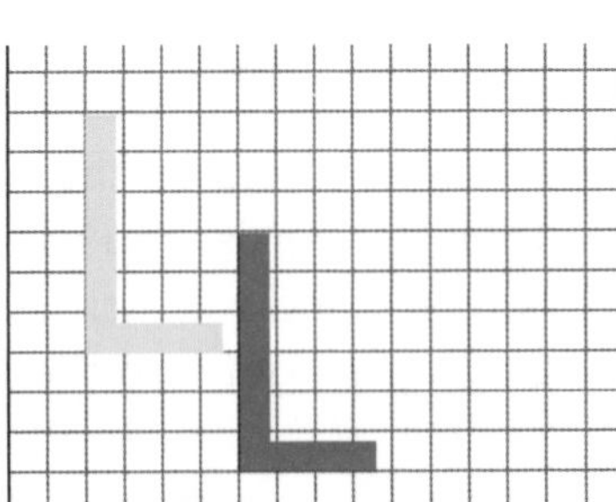

To draw a reflection accurately, imagine the line is a mirror. Draw dots on each corner of the shape and count the squares across to the mirror. This can then be mirrored so that each point is reflected.

This will help...

You may be asked about congruent shapes. Congruent just means identical – congruent shapes are the same size and shape, but in different positions.
These two triangles are congruent.

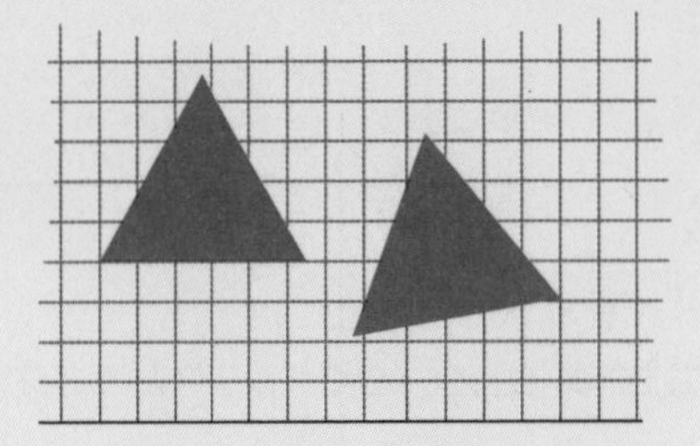

These two triangles are similar, but not congruent.

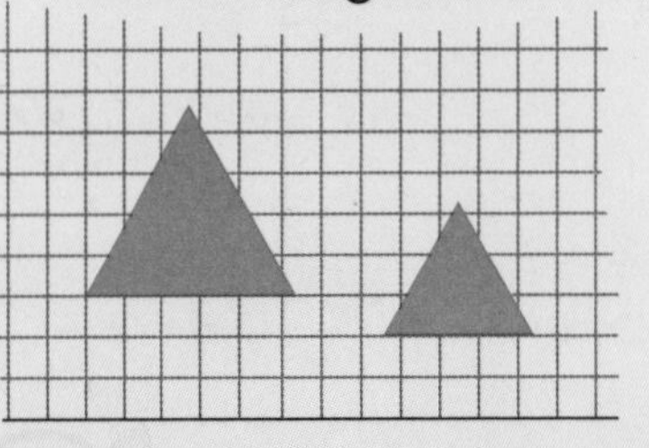

Try these

Do these shapes show a reflection, a translation or a rotation?

1 T T 2 V V

3 N N

4 Are these two shapes congruent?

Puzzle code

What is the next tile in this sequence?

  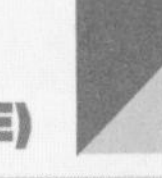 (E)  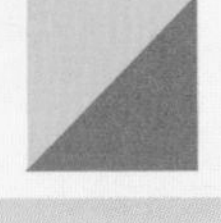 (T)  (I) (O)

Write the letter in the grid on page 64.

On your toes Which triangle has rotational symmetry of the order 3?

Coordinates

Revise wise

A co-ordinate shows an exact position of a point on a grid.

On the graph on the right the coordinates of *A* are (2, 5) and *B* are (4, 1).
What are the co-ordinates for *C*?

Co-ordinates are always written in **brackets**, separated by a comma.

Negative numbers can be used to show positions, co-ordinates:

A (−1, −4) *B* (3, −2)

C (−4, +3) *D* (2, 1)

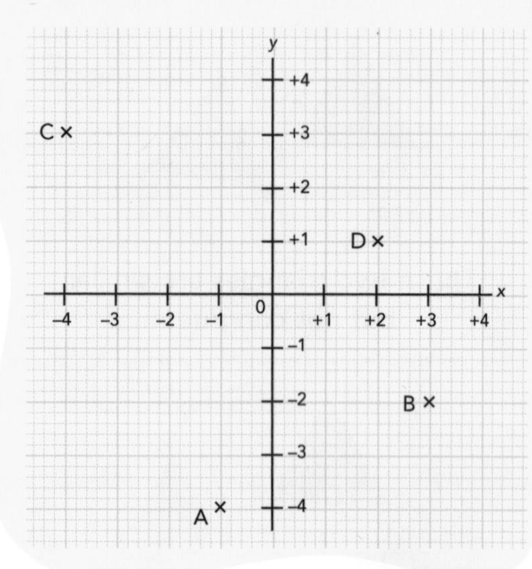

These co-ordinates are in all four **quadrants**:

4th quadrant | 1st quadrant
3rd quadrant | 2nd quadrant

This will help...

The numbers on the horizontal x-axis are written first, then the y-axis. You can remember this because x comes before y and x is a-cross (funny eh!). It is a bit like reading a graph – get into the habit of reading along the x-axis and then up to the y.

Try these

These are three corners of a rectangle.
What are the co-ordinates for:

1 *A*
2 *B*
3 *C*
4 The fourth corner

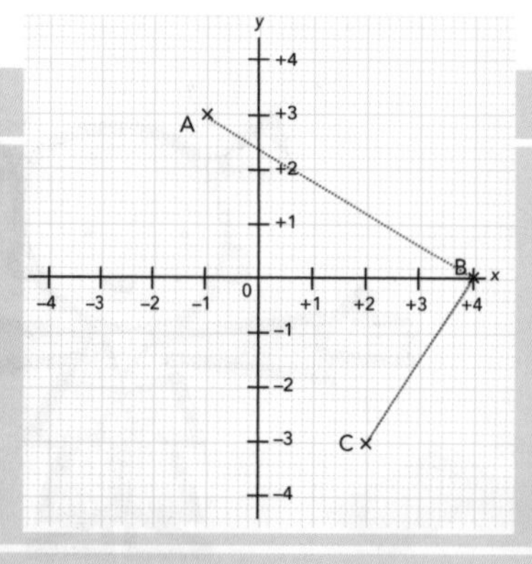

Puzzle code

If the fourth corner of the shape above was at position (0, −2), what would the new shape be?

Write the letter in the grid on page 64.

Rhombus **(T)** Kite **(R)** Trapezium **(U)** Parallelogram **(L)**

 On your toes Which is a 'slide' movement: a rotation, a translation or a reflection?

Angles

An angle is a measure of turn between two lines. Angles are measured in degrees (°).

All angles must be pretty special (there are only 360 of them…) but these are extra special so try to remember them:

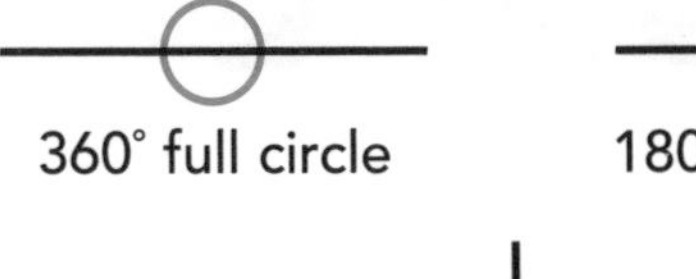
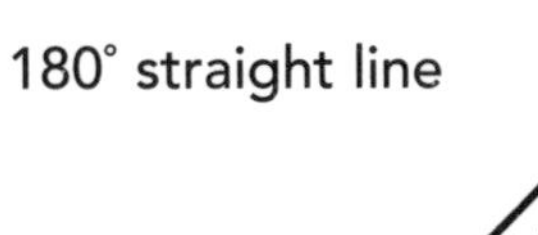

360° full circle

180° straight line

90° right angle

acute angle less than a right angle

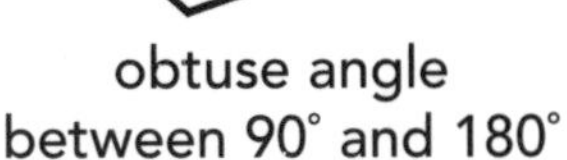
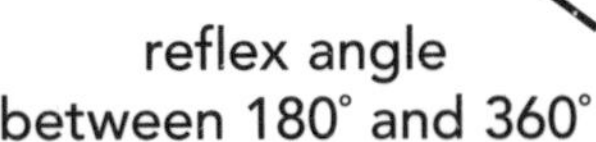

obtuse angle between 90° and 180°

reflex angle between 180° and 360°

This will help...

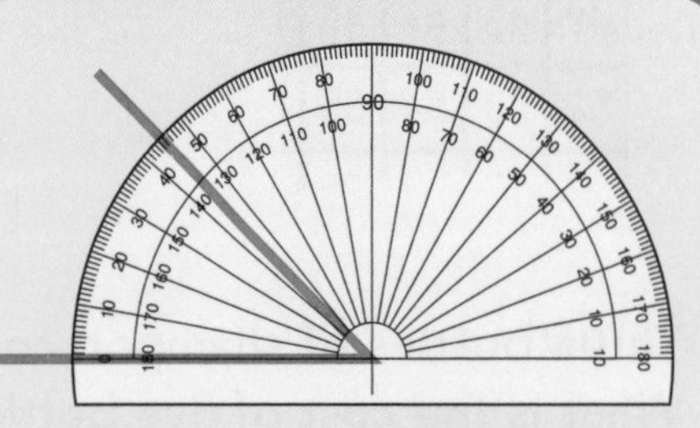

Practise using a protractor to measure the size of different angles. It is a good idea to estimate the angle first and then measure it.
Place the cross at the point of the angle you are measuring, lining up 0° on the bottom line. Then read up to the angle: this is 45°.

All the angles of a triangle add up to 180°

$a + b + c = 180°$

All the angles of a quadrilateral add up to 360°

$a + b + c + d = 360°$

Here are a few more angle facts for you to try to remember:

Angles on a straight line add up to 180°

Perpendicular lines meet at 90°

Angles at a point add up to 360°

When two straight lines cross, the opposite angles are equal

Try these

1 Is this an obtuse or a reflex angle?

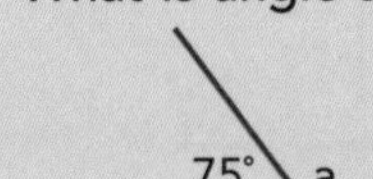

2 What do the angles of a parallelogram total?

3 What is the missing angle?

4 What is angle a?

Measure the turn from a point in degrees

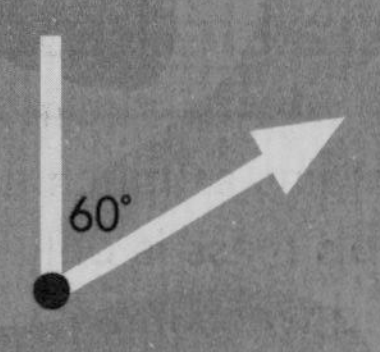

Puzzle code

What is the size of angle a?

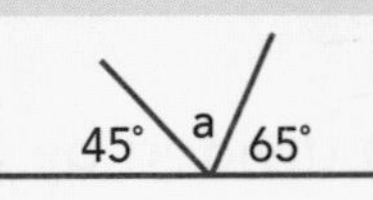

60° (T) 75° (N) 80° (L) 70° (S)

Write the letter in the grid on page 64.

On your toes Which is the x-axis and which is the y-axis?

Test questions

1 Circle two numbers that total 99.

32	33	34	35	3
42	43	44	45	
52	53	54	55	

2 Three bottles of shampoo cost £3.75.
What is the cost of five bottles of shampoo?
Show your working in the box below.

3 This is a centimetre square grid.
What is the area of the triangle?

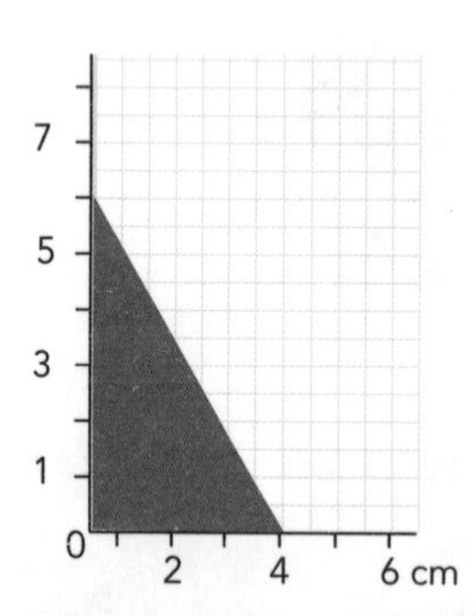

4 A set of number cards 1 to 20 is shuffled and the top card turned over.
Tick the box on the scale that shows the probability of turning over a multiple of 3.

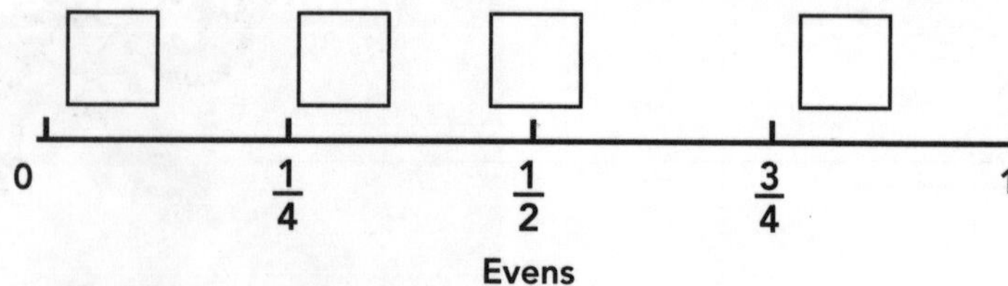

5 Circle the number that has a remainder of 2 when divided by 3.

145 217 650 411 505

6 What are the co-ordinates for point A? (______ , ______)
Draw the reflection of the shape in the mirror line.
You may use tracing paper or a mirror.

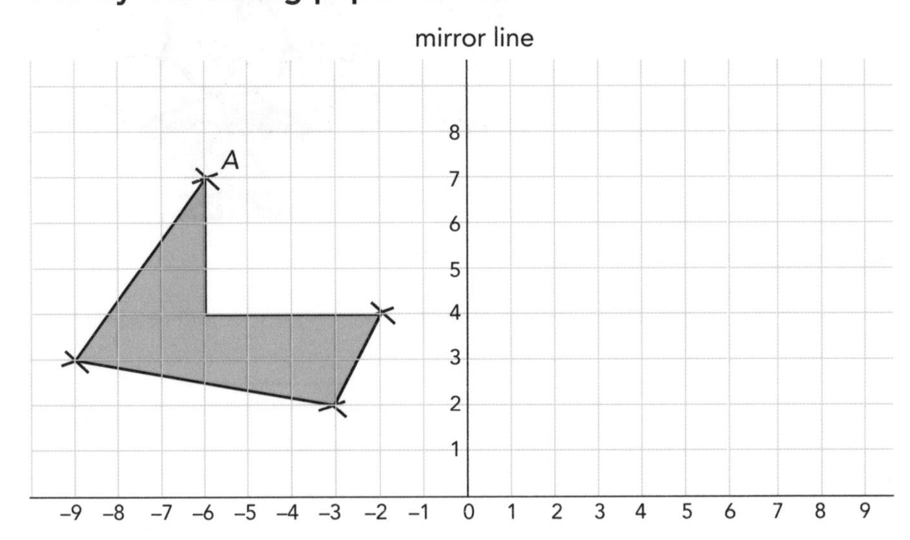

7 Use these four cards to make the number as near as possible to 60.

8 The 1355 train from Nottingham to Manchester is 12 minutes late leaving Nottingham.
It is a 1 hour 15 minute journey. What time does it arrive at Manchester?

9 Jim has a collection of 120 medals.
He buys some boxes which each hold 26 medals. How many boxes will he need to store his collection?
Show your working in the box below.

10 Write two possible missing numbers.

$(64 - \square) \times \square = 200$

11 Write a fraction that could go in the missing space.

$\frac{1}{5} < \square < \frac{3}{4}$

12 Calculate $936 \div 8$

Show your working in the box below.

13 This pie chart shows the different crops grown on a farm.
What percentage of the crops is barley?

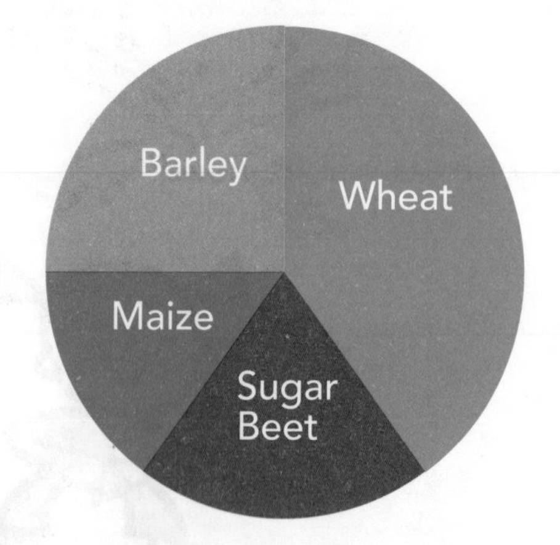

14 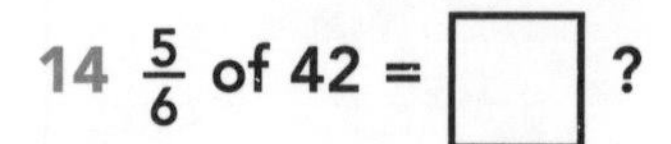

$\frac{5}{6}$ of 42 = $\square$?

15 This table shows the goals scored by Midtown United in their first 10 matches.

Game	1	2	3	4	5	6	7	8	9	10
Goals Scored	3	4	2	5	1	0	1	3	6	4

What is the mean number of goals scored?
Round this to the nearest whole number.

16 What is 15% of £9?
Show your working in the box below.

17 What is the value of the missing angle?

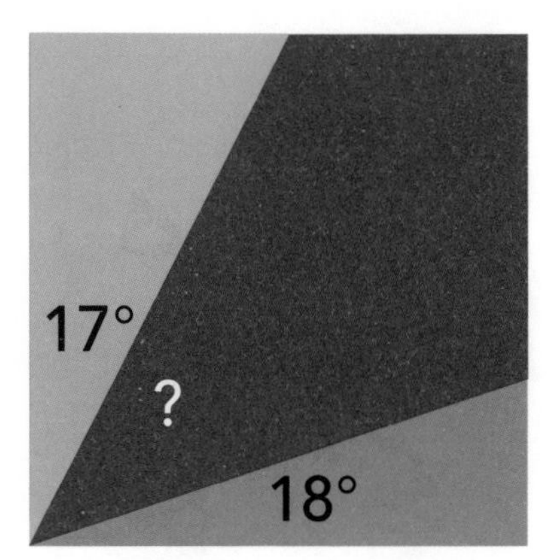

18 Circle the fraction that is not equivalent to $\frac{2}{5}$.

$\frac{20}{50}$ $\frac{4}{10}$ $\frac{12}{40}$ $\frac{6}{15}$ $\frac{18}{45}$

19 This shows a calendar for a sponsored cycle ride by Steve Jones.

May

Mon	Tues	Weds	Thurs	Fri	Sat	Sun
4	5	6	7 Start cycle race	8	9	10
11	12	13	14	15	16	17 Finish cycle race
18	19	20	21	22	23	24
25	26	27	28	29	30	31

He cycles a distance of 65km each day. Put a cross on the day he passes 500km.
How far does he travel in total?
He is sponsored for £20 for every kilometre he cycles. How much does he raise altogether?
Show your working in the box below.

20 Calculate 619×35.
Show your working in the box below.

21 The rule for this number pattern is ■ = 2 × ▲ + 1.
Write in the missing numbers.

▲	3	4	5	6	7
■	7				15

22 This shape turns clockwise 90° around point X.
Draw the new position of the shape.
You may use tracing paper.

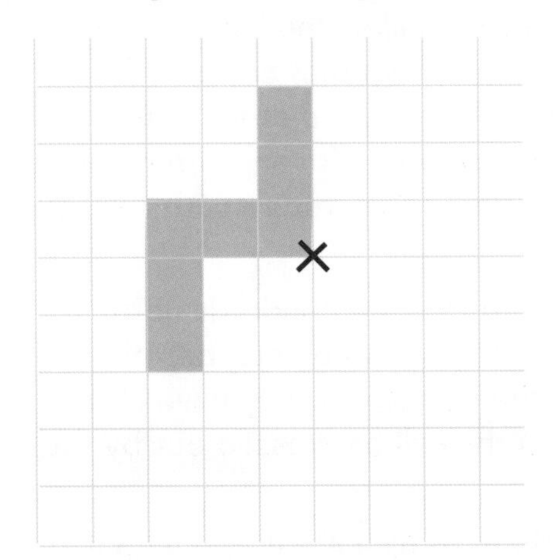

Beyond the book

In the home

- **Cooking** – ask your child to get some partly-used items, such as cereal, flour, sugar, dried fruit pasta, rice, from the cupboards. They should look at the weight on the packet and estimate how much is left, then weigh the amount left. *How much has been used? Is there enough flour if you need 250 g to make a cake?*
- **Breakfast cereal** – ask your child to pour out a bowl of cereal. *What is the mass? How many more bowls of cereal will you get from the amount left? How many bowls would you get from a whole packet? Do you eat more or less than the typical serving suggested on the packet?*
- **Watching TV** – your child should find the time a programme starts. *What time is it now? How long before the programme starts? What time does the next programme begin? So how long is the programme?* Setting a video often involves using 24-hour time so give them the opportunity to record programmes.
- **Shapes around the house** – ask your child to think of a shape that they have seen in the house. They give 3 clues, so that you can guess the shape and the object. Switch round and you give three details of a shape for your child to guess. For example, *The shape I'm thinking of is a 3D shape, it has two circle faces and a curved face. It is in the kitchen.* How many more clues are needed to guess correctly?

In the car

- **Multiplying number plates** – *what is the value of the car in front? Multiply the 3 digits.* Take turns to see who makes the highest number. Alternatively ask your child to multiply them together and play as a game, *Odds against evens.* One player is 'evens', the other 'odds'. Take turns and play it like tennis. The first player 'serves' with an even number, and the other player must return with an odd number. If they return with an even the other player gets the points. Scoring can be like tennis.
- **Rounding numbers** – at the start of the journey ask your child to write hundreds up to 1000 (100, 200, 300...), on a piece of paper. They can look for 3-digit numbers on number plates that round to the nearest hundred. Then they can cross out the number as they have been used. For example, 2 5 0 rounds to 300 so cross this out. Can they all be crossed out by the end of the journey?
- **Car Bingo** – this is for more than one child in the car, ask them to fill a 4 × 4 grid with any 3 digit numbers ending in zero, e.g. 410, 380, 500. As they travel along, play bingo by crossing out the numbers as they see plate numbers rounded to their nearest tens. The first to cross them all out is the winner.

In the shops

- **Estimating weights** – ask your child to select fruit and vegetables. How close can they get to 500 g – apples, tomatoes…? How close to 1 kg? Use different food for practice.
  Lift a bag of flour, box of cereal, loaf of bread… 'Feel' the weight and make an estimate. How close were they?
- **Guess the total** – when buying a list of items, round prices to the nearest £1 or 10 p. It is better to start in a shop where they can only buy up to five items, such as a newsagents or a chemists. How do you choose which is best – rounding to 10 p or £1? If they are confident, try rounding for a small supermarket shop. Consider that it might be easier with more items to round to the nearest £1. After a big supermarket shop each can have a guess as to the total cost.
- **Bargain hunting** – ask your child to look for price offers around the shops. *Which is the best value?* For example 500 g pack for £3.50 or 400 g pack for £2.40? Work out the price of 100 g first, for both. *What is the cost of one item when you buy one and get the second half price? What is the price of the CD if there is a 20% sale?*

Rainy days

- **Domino multiples** – use a set of dominoes. Ask your child to make a domino square where the total of each side is a multiple of 5. The joining dominoes need not match. They can make different domino squares for multiples of 5 and explore other multiples.
- **Playing Card totals** – using just the 1-10 diamonds make sets of cards to total 15. How many cards can you use up? Using any 3 cards make the total 20, how many ways can you do this? Using 6 cards how many different ways can you make 50?
- **Guess the number** – select a number playing card. Ask what number you have. Give clues one at a time, for example its an odd number, it is a prime number, it is greater than 6. *Can you name this card in one?* Extend this to any number to 100 or 1000.
- **Sweet sort** – ask your child to use a packet of sweets such as chews or Smarties and lay them out on the table. They can arrange them in columns as a simple graph to show the different flavours or colours. *What fraction is red? What fraction is lemon flavour? What is the ratio of red to yellow in the pack. What proportion of the pack is green? What is the probability of picking a blackcurrant flavour?*

Answers

Place value

Page 2

1 Ninety-two thousand and thirty-four

2 120 604

3 64 100

4 Two thousand

Puzzle code O

Odd one out 62 374 (all the others have the same digits)

On your toes 1001

10s, 100s and 1000s

Page 3

1 31 400

2 602

3 1000

4 47 100

Puzzle code N

Odd one out 611 000

On your toes 607 318

Comparing numbers

Page 4

1 769 1809 1997 7066 7645

2 14 006

3 >

4 Any three numbers greater than 62 121 and smaller than 62 110

Puzzle code C

Odd one out 90 123 < 9300 (the sign is wrong)

On your toes 121 030 km

Approximating numbers

Page 5

1 £43 700

2 36 000g

3 Approximately 328 500

4 Approximately 10 700

Puzzle code E

Odd one out 5765 → 5770 (the others round to the nearest 100, this is rounded to the nearest 10)

On your toes 3800

Negative numbers

Page 6

1 −10°C, −6°C, 0°C, 4°C, 17°C

2 10

3 −3, −1

4 −4

Puzzle code Y

Odd one out −7, −3, 1, 5, 9, 13, 17 (these have a difference of 4, the other rows have a difference of 3)

On your toes 218 000 km^2

Number sequences

Page 7

What's next? 4, 23, 96, 49

1 47

2 −9

3 9 and 31

4 77

Puzzle code O

Odd one out 58, 62, 66, 70, 74, 78 (the rule is +4, the rule for the other rows is +5)

On your toes 15°C

Multiples

Page 8

1 64

2 No

3 141, 144

4 Yes

Puzzle code U

Odd one out 136 (all the others can be divided by 3)

On your toes 19

Factors

Page 9

1 1, 20, 2, 10, 4, 5

2 No

3 Yes

4 7

Puzzle code H

Odd one out 9 (all the others are prime numbers)

On your toes 92 and 96

Revise wise

Special numbers

Page 10

1 121
2 64
3 yes
4 9
Puzzle code A
Odd one out 15 (all the others are square numbers)
On your toes 1, 36, 2, 18, 3, 12, 4, 9, 6

Fractions

Page 11

1 $\frac{3}{5}$
2 check drawing shows $\frac{7}{8}$
3 $\frac{15}{20}$
4 $\frac{2}{5}$
Puzzle code V
Odd one out $\frac{7}{24}$
(all the others are equivalent to $\frac{1}{3}$)
On your toes 144

Comparing fractions

Page 12

1 $\frac{11}{12}$, $\frac{7}{12}$, $\frac{3}{12}$, $\frac{1}{12}$
2 $\frac{2}{5}$
3 $\frac{1}{4}$, $\frac{3}{8}$, $\frac{5}{8}$, $\frac{3}{4}$
4 Less
Puzzle code E
On your toes $\frac{3}{4}$

Fractions of quantities

Page13

1 8
2 15
3 120 ml
4 £1.35
Puzzle code F
Odd one out 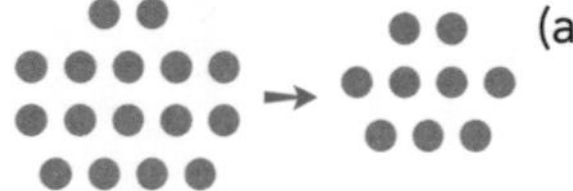 (all the rest have $\frac{1}{2}$)
On your toes $\frac{3}{4}$

Ratio and proportion

Page 14

1 12 oranges
2 $\frac{1}{2}$
3 6
4 1:2
Puzzle code I
On your toes 45

Decimal notation

Page 15

1 0.3
2 0.04
3 $\frac{7}{100}$
4 7.29
Puzzle code N
Odd one out 17.03 (all the others have the same value)
On your toes 12

Decimal places

Page 16

1 0.623
2 0.8
3 100
4 3.6
Puzzle code I
Odd one out 2.7 → 0.72
(all the others are divided by 10)
On your toes 7 (hundredths)

Ordering decimals

Page 17

1 1.07, 1.7, 2.8, 2.99, 3.04
2 9.2
3 <
4 Any number between 1.6 and 1.71
Puzzle code S
Odd one out 1.29 > 1.3
(1.29 is not greater than 1.3, all the others are true)
On your toes 1.38

Rounding decimals

Page 18

1 35 kg

2 £138.50

3 Approximately 24 (rounding to nearest whole numbers)

4 Approximately 4.6 (rounding to nearest tenth)

Puzzle code H

Odd one out 3.641 → 3.7 (this has been incorrectly rounded)

On your toes 9.4

Decimals and fractions

Page 19

1 $\frac{4}{5}$

2 0.07

3 $\frac{1}{3}$

4 $\frac{84}{100}$ or $\frac{21}{25}$

Puzzle code E

Odd one out 0.4 → $\frac{2}{5}$ (it is the only correct answer)

On your toes 28.4 litres

Percentages

Page 20

1 $\frac{7}{20}$

2 90%

3 90%

4 $\frac{17}{25}$

Puzzle code D

Odd one out $\frac{1}{4}$

(all the others are the same)

On your toes 0.04

Percentages of amounts

Page 21

1 £1.00

2 200

3 £3.20

4 68

Puzzle code T

On your toes 60%

Number facts

Page 22

1	18	36	49	48
2	15	11	13	14
3	7	4	9	7
4	5	7	7	9

Puzzle code H

Odd one out 15 + 7 (all the others have the same answer)

On your toes £85.50

Mental addition

Page 23

1 123

2 91

3 126

4 2150

Puzzle code I

Odd one out 29 + 46 (all the others have the same answer)

On your toes 15 − 7

Written addition

Page 24

1 4401

2 313.76

3 10 247

4 £1630.05

Puzzle code S

Odd one out 426 + 419 (all the others have the same answer)

On your toes 131

Mental subtraction

Page 25

1 44

2 37

3 5.2

4 £3.52

Puzzle code B

Odd one out 96 − 41 (all the others have the same answer)

On your toes 15924

Written subtraction

Page 26

1 2428

2 73.46

3 1767

4 6.62 kg

Puzzle code O

Odd one out 38.6 − 18.93 (all the others have the same answer)

On your toes 7.7

Mental multiplication

Page 27

1 273

2 They both have the same answer 264

3 344g

4 £3.48

Puzzle code O

Odd one out 66 x 7 (all the others have the same answer)

On your toes 4369m

Written multiplication

Page 28

1 4704

2 1620

3 £24.36

4 21 390

Puzzle code K

Odd one out 160 × 15 (all the others have the same answer)

On your toes more

Mental division

Page 29

1 7

2 13

3 70

4 33

Puzzle code Y

Odd one out $\frac{81}{9}$ (all the others have the same answer)

On your toes more

Written division

Page 30

1 93

2 626 r 3

3 £146.50

4 156.5

Puzzle code O

Odd one out 74 ÷ 3 (all the others have a remainder of 1)

On your toes yes

Using a calculator

Page 31

1 £86.70

2 19

3 183

4 £51.30

Puzzle code U

On your toes 2

Problem solving

Page 32

1 £1.85

2 £1.80

3 4 weeks and 5 days

4 244

Puzzle code W

On your toes £10.50

Formulae and equations

Page 33

1 $t = 5$

2 16

3 $b = 30$

4 $c = 8$

Puzzle code I

Odd one out $15 + 2a = 3$ (4 is the value of the letters in all the others)

On your toes £1.14

Money

Page 34

1 £7487

2 £189.60

3 £6.89

4 £44.23

Puzzle code L

Odd one out £2.81 (each of the others total to £2.72)

On your toes $n = 7$

Probability

Page 35

1 1 in 3 or $\frac{1}{3}$

2 1 in 2 or $\frac{1}{2}$ or 50% or 50:50

3 2 in 3 or $\frac{2}{3}$

4 1 in 6 or $\frac{1}{6}$

Puzzle code L
On your toes £52.47

Graphs and charts

Page 36

1 65
2 $\frac{1}{4}$
3 between 50 and 60
4 60
Puzzle code B
On your toes 50%, 0.5, 1 in 2 or $\frac{1}{2}$ chance

Line graphs

Page 37

1 5 m
2 4 gallons
3 45 mins
4 175 km
Puzzle code E
On your toes a record of 'how many' of something.

Mode, median and mean

Page 38

1 The range is 5 (between sizes 4 and 9).
2 8
3 8
4 7
Puzzle code A
Odd one out range (all the others are types of averages)
On your toes miles per hour

Length

Page 39

1 0.25 km
2 85 mm
3 Approximately 80 km per hour
4 Approximately 15 cm
Puzzle code M
Odd one out 4.25m (all the others are the same length)
On your toes 10 m

Mass

Page 40

1 2040 g
2 0.8 kg
3 240g
4 100 kg
Puzzle code A
Odd one out 6kg 50g (all the others are the same weight)
On your toes Approximately 9-10 m

Capacity

Page 41

1 6.8 l
2 2350 ml or 235cl
3 7 pints
4 3650 ml
Puzzle code T
Odd one out 7 litres 25ml (all the others are the same)
On your toes 1350 g or 1.35 kg

Perimeter and area

Page 42

1 63 cm^2
2 32 cm
3 24 cm^2
4 24 cm
Puzzle code H
On your toes approximately 3

Reading the time

Page 43

1 8.55 or five minutes to nine
2 20:55
3 1 hour 2 mins or 62 minutes
4 4 hours 41 mins
Puzzle code S
Odd one out The clockface showing 7.43 (the others show 7.47)
On your toes 28 cm (each side is 7 cm)

2D shapes

Page 44

1 parallelogram
2 isosceles
3 6
4 All sides and angles are equal

Puzzle code G

Odd one out the pentagon (all the others are quadrilaterals)

On your toes 1 hour and 32 minutes

3D shapes

Page 45

1 tetrahedron (triangular-based pyramid)
2 cylinder
3 8
4 triangular prism

Puzzle code E

Odd one out cone (all the others are polyhedra)

On your toes rhombus

Symmetry

Page 46

1 2
2 2
3 2
4 2

Puzzle code N

Odd one out F (all the others have are symmetrical)

On your toes 8

Moving shapes

Page 47

1 rotation
2 reflection or translation
3 translation
4 yes

Puzzle code I

On your toes equilateral triangle

Coordinates

Page 48

1 (−1, 3)
2 (4, 0)
3 (2, −3)
4 (−3, 0)

Puzzle code U

On your toes translation

Angles

Page 49

1 reflex
2 360°
3 35°
4 105°

Puzzle code S

On your toes x-axis is horizontal, y-axis is vertical

Test questions

1 circle either 45 and 54 or 44 and 55
2 £6.25, check working shows three stages
3 12cm^2
4 $\frac{3}{10}$ (between $\frac{1}{4}$ and $\frac{1}{3}$)
5 650
6 (-6, 7) check drawing, it may help to use a mirror
7 58.63
8 1522
9 5 boxes, check working
10 Check the numbers give the correct answer. Answer could be -14 and 40
11 Check the fraction is larger than $\frac{1}{5}$ but smaller than $\frac{3}{4}$. The answer could be $\frac{1}{2}$.
12 117
13 25%
14 35
15 3
16 £1.35
17 55°
18 $\frac{12}{40}$
19 a Thursday 14th **b** 715 **c** £14 300
20 21 665
21 9 11 13
22

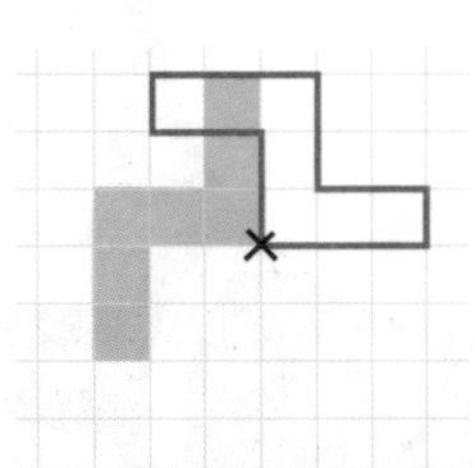

Puzzle code

As you use this book, work out the correct answer to the puzzle code questions on each page.

Write the corresponding letter in the right spaces below, to figure out the code.